F

When Motoring Was Fun

Early Days on the Open Road

"Transports of Delight"
Reminiscences
by

Tom Tyler

HALSGROVE

First published in Great Britain in 2008

British Library Cataloguing-in-Publication Data
A CIP record for this title is available from the British Library

ISBN 978 1 84114 765 9

HALSGROVE

Halsgrove House
Ryelands Industrial Estate
Bagley Road
Wellington
Somerset TA21 9PZ
T: 01823 653777
F: 01823 216796
e: sales@halsgrove.com
www.halsgrove.com

*Many of the images included in this book are taken from the Halsgrove Community History Series
which comprises over 180 titles published by Halsgrove in association with communities throughout Britain.
The resultant archive of images, numbering 40 000 in total to date, is an important record not
only of individual communities but of the country as a whole. More information about the
Community History Series is available at www.Halsgrove.com*

Printed in Great Britain by CPI Antony Rowe Ltd, Wiltshire

**Essex County
Council Libraries**

Contents

Admiring a Jaguar XK in the High Street in Monks Orchard, near Croydon, in the days when you could park anywhere.

Dedicated to the memory of my brother, Nicholas Tyler,
an experienced and enthusiastic driver for many years.

Bibliography

The Worlds Veteran to Vintage Cars. John Lloyd. MacDonald, London.

British Cars of the late 1930s. Ed. Bart Vanderveen. Frederick Warne.

Austin Seven. Chris Harvey. Oxford Illustrated Press.

Classic Cars. Ed. Brazendale & Aceti. Black Cat, MacDonald & Co.

British Saloon Cars of the Fifties. Michael Allen.

Observers Book of Automobiles. Ed. L.A.Manwaring. Frederick Warne.

Wonder Book of Motors. Harry Golding. Ward Lock & Co Ltd.
(This is a lovely snapshot of motoring up to the mid 1930s.)

Austin A30 and A35. 1951–62. R.M.Clarke. Brooklands Books.

One Hundred Years of Motoring. R.A.C. Books. Raymond Flower and Michael Wynn Jones.
(A very interesting book with wonderful photographs.)

Malcolm Root's Transport Paintings, and *Pageant of Transport.* Halsgrove.

Introduction

For well over a hundred years, the railway has competed with road passenger transport to take people to their chosen destinations. But you do not make jokes about the mighty train, or very seldom. The vast, powerful steam engine towers over mere mortals. In its cab a driver, blessed with great skill and experience, guides this mighty locomotive through the countryside, reading the road, keeping to a tight timetable. He is supported by a skilled and athletic fireman, providing the power for this great enterprise. A guard, invested with the flags and whistle as symbols of authority, supervises the flocks of passengers and ensures their safety. The travellers are whirled in comfort and safety from one station to another, relaxed, reading books and papers, or partaking of refreshment as supplied on the train.

With the car it is totally different. From the first they were seen as a sort of highway comic turn that would be very transient. Here today and blown up or broken down tomorrow. The driver was depicted as a travelling comedian. He had to supply fuel and all the other necessities for his chariot. He had to persuade it to start, and then move, preferably in the right direction. He had to read the road, ascending steep hills, and even worse descending them, and find his way without the benefit of rails. He might be given a map to further test his skills. He would do the work of a fireman, frequently pumping with vigour to encourage supply of some liquid or another. He would also have to look out for pieces dropping off his car on the road, avoid the worst potholes if possible, and cope with punctures and other breakdowns. He would be required to see to the safety of his passengers, making sure they did not fall out through improperly closed doors and the like.

And, as back copies of *Punch* show, he became the butt of every cartoonist and humourist in the country! It was challenge and adventure enough trying to make the journey from A to B, without being the object of mirth and ridicule in magazine and newspaper.

This book tries, with the help of old photographs and reminiscences, to take you back to the days when motoring was indeed a challenge and an adventure, and, one has to admit, did have its humourous moments. But one piece of research has fascinated me. I have looked through many of the titles of the Community History Series published by Halsgrove. Many of the photographs come from these excellent books.

It is my hope that this book, which makes no claim to be a comprehensive history of motoring, will none the less bring back happy memories of motoring in the past, and even a wry smile as recollection of some notable disaster comes to mind!

I have much enjoyed writing this book, and once again it has brought me into contact with many delightful and most helpful people. I would especially wish to mention Michael Ladd, my brother Wilfrid Tyler, and Peter Bannister and the staff at the Ipswich Transport museum for their assistance. My daughter has again set up the necessary computer programme, which is quite beyond me! And my long-suffering wife has proof read the book for me. Now she can look forward to my study being a little tidier!

Tom Tyler
2008

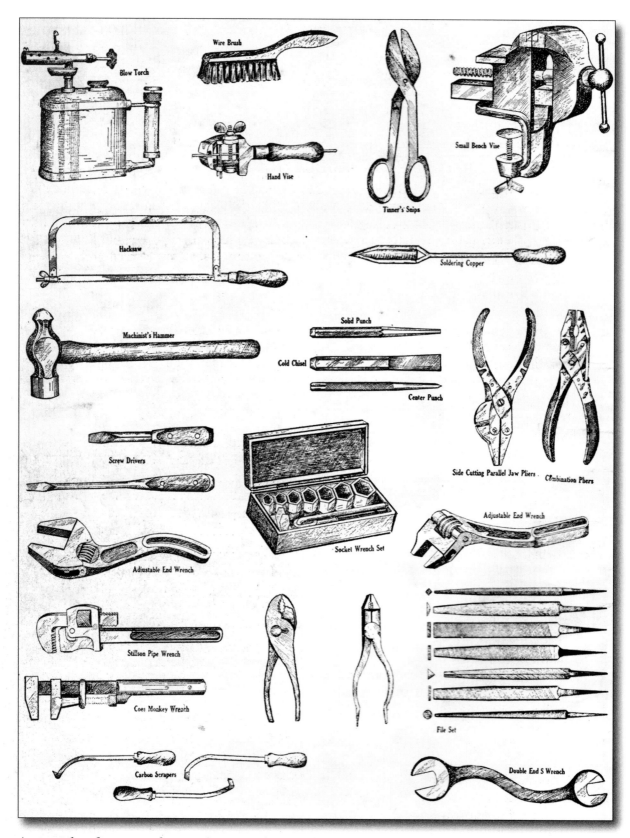

A page taken from an early motoring magazine Overhauling, Rebuilding and Repairing The Motor Car *showing 'Common tools that can be employed to advantage in overhauling an automobile power plant.'*

Chapter 1

THE FIRST TWENTY YEARS 1885 TO 1914

At the beginning, the popular name for the newly invented motor car suggested a fundamental deficiency. It was christened 'The Horseless Carriage.' For the best part of 2000 years horses had been pulling chariots, carts and carriages round Britain, in every conceivable way, and suddenly we had a carriage but no horse. What a joke! Of course doubters had been silenced before. All those who had scoffed at the railways had had to come to terms with heavy trains thundering through the countryside at nearly 100 miles per hour. But this new 'motor car' was ridiculous. It would never catch on, but probably catch fire instead. They had already had a good laugh at steam carriages, invented as far back as 1770, in France. They were very slow, constantly needed a drink, and frequently blew up. By 1850 they were more efficient, but the horse-loving opposition insisted they were preceded by a man on foot carrying a red flag, a law applied to all vehicles not pulled by a horse, and they had to pay punitive tolls on roads and bridges. These obstacles effectively drove them off the road, until 1896 when the laws were altered.

Gottlieb Daimler built the first petrol driven car in 1885. In the next ten years other makes like Panhard Levasseur in France appeared, until the first British car, an 8hp Lanchester was introduced in 1895.

But from the start there was a dilemma over design. Makers were strongly influenced by the horse-drawn carriages they were competing with. What should be the correct layout? A carriage had its horse in front, then the driver, and then the passengers. With the new horseless carriage steering had to be by the front wheels. The drive from a front-mounted engine had to be transmitted to the rear wheels, which involved lengthy and vulnerable chains or the like. Where should you put the petrol tank, away from the risk of fire? If you solved the transmission problems by putting the engine in the back, close to the rear wheels, you then had the problem of the driver's controls to the engine. Or should the driver sit in the back, with his passengers in front of him? Would he be able to see where he was going? And how would he steer the car. Reins somehow did not seem appropriate. Could he use a tiller like a boat, or would a wheel of some sort give better control?

In the event every different permutation was tried in the early years, but by 1900 the majority had settled on an engine in the front, then the driver with a steering wheel, and controls through a partition direct to the engine. Drive was taken to the back wheels. Passengers could sit beside the driver or behind him, as often was the case in a horse-drawn carriage.

Dr Bennett in his Locomobile with his daughter Myrtle. The lack of numberplate dates the car as pre-1903. Note the tiller steering.

When Motoring Was Fun

West Street, Fareham, about 1900, dominated by horse-drawn vehicles, but with a single car hiding in the background on the left of the picture.

When the railways were being built, there were many people, especially conservative country landowners, who wanted to have nothing to do with such an infernal machine! The same applied to the motor car. The machines were unreliable, smelly, gave off fumes and smoke, and were noisy and inclined to backfire, frightening the horses, by gad! There is a splendid photograph of a London bus driver trying to start his vehicle with a huge starting handle, while the driver of a passing horse drawn bus is looking at him with a huge grin on his face. Many a broken down car was pulled home by a local horse, to the chagrin of its owner. People predicted that the new motor vehicles would prove to be a curse in the long run, threatening their peaceful and orderly way of life, and bringing death and destruction, not to mention acute congestion, to their picturesque towns and villages. How right they were!

Meanwhile the designers of the new vehicles had two challenges. The first was the state of the roads. Outside towns the roads were rough and rutted, with dust in the dry weather and mud in the wet. Traction for the new cars was just one rear wheel, unlike the four powerful feet of a horse. It seemed necessary to have larger driving wheels at the rear, which in turn dictated a higher rear axle, and a higher body mounted on it. This tied in with the second challenge, to build the car body along the same lines as the carriage it was competing with, so that its general shape and accommodation would be familiar to customers.

The resulting design of many early cars meant that they were not easy to climb into, involving steps and handholds, and when loaded with driver and passengers they were often very top heavy. Given the state of the roads, and their increasing speed, more than that of a horse-drawn carriage, the result could be frequent capsizing.

On 14 November 1896 the first London to Brighton car run took place to celebrate the repeal of the 'Man with the Flag' Act, an event that has been held annually ever since. But still very few people were motor car owners and enthusiasts, and with the outbreak of the Boer War, and ensuing military disasters, followed by the death of Queen Victoria, Britain had other things on its mind. In other countries, notably France and Italy, progress was being made, though sometimes in different directions.

Early Days on the Open Road

'The first car in Lyme Regis, Dorset, a De Dion-Bouton of 1902 Vintage.

For example, the French had a marked preference for the 'vis-à-vis' seating arrangement, where passengers faced one another, two and two. This was certainly more sociable, but then two people had to travel backwards, which is not always very popular.

In Britain, Edward VII was eventually crowned, and the Boer War was brought to a reasonably successful end.

The nation set out to enjoy the Edwardian Era, and the twentieth century, and motor cars were given a terrific boost because both the King and Queen used them and enjoyed travelling in them.

The King, who was a well-built man, enjoyed being driven in a luxurious Daimler, while Queen Alexandria (mindful of the environment and global warming?) owned an elegant 1901 Columbia Electric Car. This had an American chassis and motor, but English bodywork, and must have been a joy to drive around on a sunny day, especially because it was smell-free and quiet. It is interesting to note that the first motor vehicle to exceed 100kph in 1899 was the Jamais Contente, built in France and shaped like a torpedo, and powered by electricity.

By about 1902 the three-way contest between steam, petrol and electricity was being won by the petrol engine. This had a much better range than

an electric powered vehicle, because of battery development, and a better power/weight ratio than the steam engine. There were other factors. My father drove an early steam car with a boiler under the front seat, and a gas-powered heating burner. If you passed a side street on a windy day, a sudden draught could blow out the burner, which then re-lit after a short interval from the pilot light, causing a loud explosion right under the driver's posterior. It was very unnerving!

The period between 1902 and 1914 was one of great development for the car. In Britain alone there were about 200 different car manufacturers by the outbreak of the First World War. Some had formerly made bicycles, some steam cars, some other types of engineering. Shortly Ford from the USA would establish their first overseas plant on Merseyside.

Meanwhile every conceivable variation on an Original Theme was being tried. For the ordinary motorist the family saloon could come in at least eight different body styles, from the humble 'dos-a-dos' or 'mylord', to the opulent landaulet.

As early as 1907 Herbert Austin, who was to become a most important name in the British Car industry, brought out his first 7hp Car. What was also most significant was the drop in prices for an average family car, perhaps £400 in 1900, to well under £200 for a Morris Cowley in 1914.

When Motoring Was Fun

As the use of the motor car gained momentum, householders began to build new garages to house temperamental vehicles, or to convert existing stables, no longer needed for horses and carriages.

A car was still very much a preserve of the more wealthy, and a lot of people would employ a chauffeur who could also do a spot of gardening when he was not required for a journey. But for many, mainly men it must be admitted, the fun of driving your own car was a great attraction. They were the modern knights of the road, albeit now on wheels.

However, the early motorists faced one particular challenge, and that was the elements. Some early cars had hoods of a sort. One French model was based on the surrey with the fringe on top, it had a decorative flat fabric roof with a tasteful fringe round the edges. But many of the cheaper models had nothing at all, so driver and passengers had to provide their own protection against wind, rain, snow and freezing conditions. It should be put on record that there were probably a great many fine weather motorists, and who could blame them?

This situation produced an interesting challenge for the motorist, and one which produced some fascinating fashions. There were those who put elegance first, and relied on hats, scarves and furs to keep warm. Boots of some sort were an essential. Goggles were also essential if the eyes were to be kept free of dust and mud, and some children were equipped with an all-in-one head covering which included the goggles. I am not sure how they breathed!

Men, and especially drivers, tended to cover everything they could, either with some specially designed overall garment, or with heavy coats. Caps and scarves were also employed, and driving gauntlets were vital if you did not want your hands to freeze to the steering wheel or tiller. There is many a story of the motoring party arriving at their destination with the entire car and its occupants

Chauffeur, Tom Towler, with two of the cars he drove for the Herring Family in Narborough, Norfolk, between 1900 and 1914.

Early Days on the Open Road

liberally covered in mud. It must have taken a lot of cleaning up, and you can imagine the reaction of the prospective hostess to the arrival of such a grubby set of visitors!

As early as 1899 Renault in France had produced a miniature sedan model, which looked like a small and very upright box mounted on four wheels, with a little bonnet in the front concealing the engine. By 1914 most manufacturers were much more aware of the need for passenger comfort, and enclosed cars, or provided adequate hoods, ensuring improving standards in passenger comfort.

Meanwhile there was a definite language problem developing, due to the tendency of citizens of the United States of America to call anything invented after 1776 by a different name. The motor car did indeed originate in Europe, where different languages obviously required different names. But could English terminology be standardised? Could it heck! The car became an auto, the bonnet a hood, and its boot a trunk. It would run on gas, not petrol, and be started if obstinate with a crank not a starting handle! It was all rather complicated, in particular later when some cars really did run on gas!

Another challenge for the early motorist was the lack of roadside facilities of the sort we take for granted today, especially garages at frequent intervals. The motorist, of whichever sex, needed to be a pretty competent car mechanic, and particularly to understand the complexities of the ignition system, which was always a source of problems then, and later! It was also essential to carry a spare can of petrol. For years petrol tank fuel gauges were notoriously inaccurate, usually filling you with a completely false sense of optimism until you lost power and came to a standstill, frequently in the middle of a busy town or halfway down a very narrow lane. You needed to carry a funnel as well. Cans often had a special attachment on the running board, so that the occupants of the car were not bothered by petrol fumes.

Two other important pieces of equipment that often nestled on running boards were the car's battery and spare tyres or wheels. The condition of many roads meant that punctures were a constant problem, and could be as bad as one a mile with awful roads and old tyres.

If you were now dressed up, and the car had started, you were ready to set off on your travels. It was essential to carry appropriate maps, and for at least one person travelling in the car to know how to read one! Signposts and other roadside signs were few or non-existent, and each community tended to bombard approaching drivers with information about local speed limits and dangerous hazards, coupled with dire threats of retribution for those not driving sufficiently carefully through their village. The great Rudyard Kipling began one of his most entertaining stories, 'The Village That

Dudley Ward, Liberal Candidate for Somerset, being greeted by his supporters during an election tour in 1911. The magnificent car clearly indicated the status of the politician.

When Motoring Was Fun

Drawing a great deal of local attention, two splendid Chauffeur driven Edwardian cars stop at the Anchor Hotel in Burton Bradstock, Dorset, for refreshments.

Voted the Earth was Flat', with the account of four motorists out for a spin in the country being stopped and charged with speeding by the local constable, who is hand in glove with the local magistrate, who duly fines them and gives them a lecture they do not forget!

You may just be planning a jaunt in the beautiful countryside, punctuated by lunch at a wayside hotel that has been recommended to you. In the photograph above it is the Anchor Hotel in Burton Bradstock. Others were far more adventurous, and in an old book on motoring I had as a boy, there are amazing photographs of pre-1914 cars in the Lake District. One, a Morris Cowley, is driving up Wrynose Pass, while the other, a large Rolls-Royce Tourer, is negotiating an impossible hair-pin bend on the way up Hard Knott Pass (see page 25). In both cases the so called road is nothing more than a very rough track suitable for sheep and hill walkers!

By 1914 the Car had also come into its own for a number of people to use in their work. For the doctor and the vet it could be a great advantage. It could be used as a taxi to link up with trains at the local railway station. Our photograph on the previous page shows what progress has been made when an election candidate uses a car to tour his constituency. The car is no longer seen as a dangerous radical development in the otherwise tranquil countryside, but as the sign of a man who is up to date and forward looking in his attitude to present day affairs. Worth voting for, in fact!

The development of the car was considerable during this period, and is chronicled faithfully by Ian Hay, a noted writer, in his novel *A Knight on Wheels*. Ian Hay also had a very good sense of humour, and his view of motor cars and their habits may have had quite an influence on the public perception of

Doctor Good on his rounds in Umberleigh Bridge, Devon, driving his single seater Swift of 1910.

the new vehicles. Mr Maplethorpe, the car's owner, is giving Philip a lift:

'Let me introduce you. I present Boenerges, my superb, four seated, two-cylinder, one dog power reaping machine.' Philip assisted his new and eccentric friend to disentangle Boenerges from the hedge and push him back into the road.

...Philip surveyed the various appliances on the dingy dashboard. There were two switches of the electric light variety, marked M and A, which he knew stood for Magneto and Accumulator. There was an oil reservoir, with a piston rod protruding from the top, and a glass gauge to show the oil level. Meanwhile Mr Maplethorpe, with the assistance of the starting handle, had been playing a monotonous and unmelodious tune upon his hurdy-gurdy-like engine. Presently he paused for breath.

'Boenerges takes a lot of starting up. I'll have one more go, and if that fails we will run him backwards down the hill and let the reverse in. That ought to do it'

This wonderful book was first published in 1914, and Boenerges is depicted as being already well stricken in years, so may have looked very like the car in the photograph below, which I believe is a Renault. I think this passage, and others, give us a very accurate contemporary view of the challenges and frustrations of managing a motor car in the Edwardian era, when nothing at all about travelling could be taken for granted, and many a journey had to be abandoned either because your cherished car would not start, or else broke down on the road.

While the Mr Maplethorpes of this world wrestled with their obstinate vehicles, there were others, blessed with a good deal of money and courage, who were pushing out the boundaries, and discovering just what the new cars could do. Bexhill-on-Sea in Sussex makes the slightly surprising claim to be the scene of the first race for cars in Britain in 1904. It later seemed to be famous for its population of Daf Variomatics! The race presumably took place along the seafront. Before this, racing in motor cars was banned in Britain by law.

However, other countries were much more far seeing, and it was realised that in order to catch the imagination of the public, races and endurance tests by cars were extremely good publicity. Such races on the continent took place before 1900, and soon the main manufacturers in France, Italy, Germany and Britain were competing in what were to become the Grand Prix races. Rules for engine size and overall weight were laid down, but the limits tended to be increased so that the cars got larger and ever more powerful. In some cases the head of a car manufacturing firm drove the racing entry, and there were several tragic accidents.

A very early 'fine weather only' motor car outside the Black Swan, in Homersfield, which spans the boundary between Norfolk and Suffolk, about 1900.

When Motoring Was Fun

Aileen and Hugh Chamberlin and their daughter, Nancy, from Mylor, Cornwall, in their dark green 15hp Star, first registered in April 1909.

One of the definite advantages of the races was that motor car technology was rapidly advanced, to the benefit of the ordinary car.

In Italy, in 1901, driving tests and licenses were laid down by law. In Britain there was no such requirement. The magazine *Truth* declared in 1899 'It is impossible to understand why a motorist should be tested before being allowed to drive a car, which can be easily controlled and does not have any speed of its own, while any scoundrel is at liberty to drive, without any test whatsoever, a strange animal with its own will and no brakes!' Compulsory driving tests were not required in Britain until 1934, which is amazing!

It is true that driving motor cars was largely a man's preserve at this time, but not entirely so, as the photograph above shows. There were some enterprising lady drivers who quickly discovered the fun of driving, and again Ian Hay, in one of his novels details the exploits of one of these lady drivers, and especially her technique for enticing passing gentlemen motorists to change her wheel for her when she got the inevitable puncture! She would sit in the road beside her stricken car, and peck hopelessly at the wheel with a tyre lever. Being a very attractive young lady, she soon had a team of male motor mechanics doing her dirty work for her, and delighted to be rewarded by her smile and grateful thanks when the job was done. Her husband and other passengers meanwhile hid in the nearby wood and much enjoyed watching the proceedings!

The 1909 Star in the photograph above is a typical car of this period. The body work is very upright, with no attempt to reduce wind resistance. It does have a fairly adequate hood, but there must have been a large gap between the front of the hood and the top of the windscreen, which would let in a lot of air and water in inclement weather.

The wheels are as usual based on carriage design, with wooden spokes and rim, and the air valves can be clearly seen. On the running board is the spare wheel. Lights on the early cars could be gas lamps, or else paraffin lamps. The latter could easily blow out in a sudden gust of wind, and there was no means of knowing if your rear light was still functioning. If it wasn't, you could be sure of being stopped by a policeman and warned of the problem.

During this period, then, the motor car made its appearance and served its apprenticeship, so to speak. It came through with flying colours, though some very useful lessons regarding safety and reliability were learned on the way. The car also began to build a whole tradition of folklore and humour all its own. Its arrival added colour to many lives, and provided amazing stories to share over a pint in the pub of an evening, always assuming that your car managed to get you to the rendezvous with your friends!

Chapter 2

TRANSPORT IN THE GREAT WAR 1914-1918

Hundreds of these buses, a familiar sight on the streets of London in the early 1900s, were shipped to France during the Great War to transport troops from area to area.

For those soldiers trying to make progress through the mud of Flanders, dead tired after a long spell up at the front, any passing form of wheeled transport which stopped to give them a lift was not so much a transport of delight as a transport of relief.

Mobility has always been a vital requirement for any army. It was pure tactical vision which led the Romans to build their network of straight, paved roads in every country they conquered. They knew how vital it was to move troops swiftly from one part of a country to another. Napoleon achieved many of his most notable victories by suddenly appearing where he was not expected. The use of horses and horse drawn wagons and horse drawn guns gave the British army a great advantage in many parts of the globe.

The First World War was a big challenge. From the outset huge numbers of men were called up to fight, and a massive German army was only halted by an equally huge Allied one.

Then the situation took a completely new twist. Both sides 'dug in' until the lines of trenches stretched from the North Sea to the Swiss frontier. These trenches were covered by artillery and machine guns, both now remarkably efficient, and it was a very unhealthy pastime to get out of your trench for any purpose whatever. But no vehicle, be it car, bus, lorry or horse-drawn vehicle could progress along a narrow trench, so the vehicles moved across a devastated countryside, making them easy to spot. Moreover, none of these vehicles could begin to withstand a direct hit from an artillery shell. To start with, they were also very vulnerable to machine gun fire, especially from a heavy machine gun. It was only later, as the war developed, that ideas for defending vehicles from the impact of machine gun bullets became a practical reality, as we shall see.

Meanwhile, troops had to be transported to the front. The journey would start in a smart family car perhaps, the father taking the warrior son to the

Giving the horses a lift at British Army manoeuvres c.1920.

local station, and then trains, a ferry, and another train in France. Finally the troops would leave their trains, and an ex-London Bus would be waiting to take them to the rest or training area, where they would be prepared during a minimum period of time for front line duty. The final journey would be on foot, up increasingly narrow supply trenches, and with shells bursting around them, to give them a flavour of what was to come. They would be passed at frequent intervals by stretcher bearers going in the opposite direction, carrying their sad and gory burdens. By the time the men reached the front line, all semblances of 'jingoism' would have completely disappeared.

Then there was the situation regarding horses. C.S. Forrester, in his book *The General* tells of the cavalry commander arriving with his cherished regiment behind the front lines in the early days of the war, and being very abruptly told to send his horses to the rear and get dug in as an attack was imminent. My Uncle Roland, living in India, joined the local Yeomanry Regiment, the Calcutta Light Horse. His only problem was that being merely a humble clerk he could not afford a horse! When they arrived in France to take part in the war, Roland was made the regimental dispatch rider, and given a motorcycle as a mark of shame. However, his comrades very quickly had to give up their horses and man the trenches, while Roland, the most mobile

man in the Regiment, miraculously survived the whole war. Dispatch riders, as a rule, did not have a long life in France because they were always messing about on the skyline, and a perfect target for a sniper's bullet.

In the photograph above, which may date from just after the war, judging from the tracked vehicle, an army lorry of First World War date is giving a lift to the local cavalry. This picture is a clear indication of what was to come in warfare in the future, but the cavalry have not accepted it gracefully. For the horses it must have come as a considerable relief!

It must be said that in the appalling conditions of Flanders' mud, vehicles could easily become bogged down, especially as the roads were at best primitive pavé, and at worst a succession of shell craters full of mud and water. There was usually a ready supply of somewhat reluctant manpower to push vehicles out of the mud, but it was not a favourite occupation of already muddy and extremely tired Tommies.

Where off-road travelling had to be done, such as when a battery of field artillery needed to be deployed and concealed from prying eyes, there was no substitute for horses, who could get a good grip on rough and slippery ground. This situation continued until the arrival of powerful and tracked artillery tractors, or wheeled vehicles with four-wheel drive.

Another fundamental requirement of the First World War army was reliable communications, and

Early Days on the Open Road

Dispatch rider with pigeons leaving for the firing line. His Majesty's Pigeon Service, November 1917.

at this point the radio was not sufficiently developed to supply the need. The alternative was field telephones, but as Ian Hay has chronicled, these too were often unreliable, the voices being drowned by a background cacophony of strange noises, or else the whole line down and out because a shell had landed close to a cable, which was usually laid on the surface.

One of the attempted solutions to this problem was the employment of racing pigeons as seen in the photograph above. They were ferried around in a converted lorry, which looks very impressive, and they must have been the smallest of His Majesty's loyal troops. The lorry must have remained stationary so that the homing pigeons could find their way back to it. Dispatch riders, as shown in the picture, then carried the pigeons in boxes on their backs to the troops up in the front line. Messages could then be sent back to headquarters. It is not recorded how reliable the pigeon post proved to be, though there is a fascinating exhibition at Bletchley Park showing how it all worked.

The Blackadder version, where the pigeon carrying very unwelcome news goes from headquarters to the front, and is shot and eaten by Blackadder, is not rooted in fact! Incidentally it is not my Uncle Roland on the motorcycle, but it easily might have been!

I believe the lorry shown is an early Thorney-croft, but even with a magnifying glass I cannot be

certain. Again, the lorry needed to keep out of range of enemy artillery or there would have been feathers everywhere.

One of the greatest, and most tragic challenges was dealing with the floods of casualties, especially during an attack on the enemy lines. Incredibly brave medical orderlies, often so called 'conscientious objectors', would go out into no-man's land and recover the wounded who would be carried on stretchers down the supply trenches to the nearest point that an ambulance could reach. The First World War ambulances were pretty primitive vehicles, often converted vans, or small lorries, and many of them were driven by women like my cousin Catherine Hitch, who can only have been 18 years old in 1916. She survived to tell the tale, but artillery shells cannot recognise ambulances, even with large red crosses painted on their sides and roofs, and many of these brave young women were killed while they tried to save the lives of others.

I feel one should mention the work of the Royal Army Service Corps and the Royal Ordnance Corps. As this appalling war scooped up more and more men, so supplies were increasingly important. The British army got the reputation of being the best fed army in the world, and this was largely due to the

First World War lorries taking part in a training exercise on Salisbury Plain.

R.A.S.C. with their ever-increasing fleet of lorries. They did at times ferry passengers as well, but they were true transports of delight for the hungry troops. Every make of lorry was pressed into service, and at times the mechanics were hard put to keep them on the road, or in the mud!

Many of the great battles of the First World War were preceded by mighty artillery barrages, and to provide these, enormous quantities of heavy shells had to be delivered to the guns. This was a huge challenge for the R.O.C. and again the use of lorries made the task much easier, although rough ground and heavy cargoes would often defeat a lorry which basically drove on one powered rear wheel.

During the war, many men applied themselves to one great challenge, which was a matter of life or death. Both machine guns and artillery became more lethal as the war progressed. What was required for vehicles was some sort of protection for drivers and passengers. There is evidence that some drivers did try to tack on pieces of metal to give themselves a little protection, at least from shrapnel and a stray snipers' bullet. There were more organised attempts to produce an 'armoured' car, but the main problem was weight, with narrow wheels and underpowered vehicles. Any metal protection which would stop a machine gun bullet was going to be a heavy addition. Real development of an effective armoured car would not come for a number of years after the war.

Meanwhile, one should mention one other very significant battlefield arrival, the tank. This British invention arose directly from the ideas of soldiers trying to work out a way to cross no-man's land in relative safety. The key to its success was the tracks,

able to cope with the mud and shell craters, and the general design which enabled it to cross trenches and other reasonable obstacles. Conditions inside the tank were dreadful, noisy and fume-ridden, and the firepower of its guns was very limited, but it was an awe-inspiring start, and it gave a huge boost to Allied morale. Infantry could shelter behind it when advancing, and even ride on it in certain circumstances, though not in the presence of enemy fire if they were wise!

John Piper of South Brent, Devon, with his lorry during the 1914–18 war.

Early Days on the Open Road

Civilians with War Department vehicles outside the Town Hall in Wilton, Wiltshire, c.1915.

Senior officers made use of staff cars, usually driven by soldiers, and these helped mobility, though it must be said that some preferred their horses throughout the war. The dreadful conditions encountered in Flanders led to rapid development of vehicles in every respect, and especially more powerful engines.

On the Home Front there were also great changes. Here two important factors influenced motoring. First, the requirements of a country geared up totally for war. Second, a severe lack of fuel for cars used for social and domestic purposes.

The First World War swallowed men at a tragic and disastrous rate. There was always a desperate need for more reinforcements, and the training of soldiers, and sailors and airmen, was cut to a bare minimum. Some would say it was criminally short, but then the times were truly desperate, and the Americans had not yet decided to give assistance.

Motor transport enabled men to be ferried to and from training areas like Salisbury Plain, as the photo opposite shows. This saved men marching everywhere, and speeded up training programmes, though it may have given the recruits a false sense of comfort! They would do plenty of marching, in awful conditions, when they got to France.

Motor transport was also vital in supplementing the railways and moving supplies to the ports, both food and munitions. A lorry could pick up a load from the production factory, which might be quite remote as everyone was geared to the war effort, and deliver it straight to the docks for onward shipment. This saved a good deal of labour and time, and was, incidentally, a foretaste of things to come.

Apart from the armed forces, there was another army of those engaged on vital war work. These included politicians, company directors, workers in factories, and also, it must be sadly recorded, a number of men who did not fancy joining their friends and relatives overseas, and who procured for themselves nice safe jobs doing 'important war

A driver poses in front of his First World War staff car.

92nd Field Company, Royal Engineers, number 1 section, in France or in training?

work' which meant they could avoid conscription. Some managed quietly to make a fortune while doing so.

In many parts of the country, and especially in London, there were wealthy people who employed chauffeurs, either because they hadn't a clue how to drive or maintain a car themselves, or else because it made busy lives a bit easier when one was driven by someone else. Many of these men volunteered for service in the army, and were eagerly grabbed because of their knowledge of motor transport and skill as drivers.

This left significant gaps, and in some cases the wives of these men took over their husband's work to keep the job safe until after the war. In London they banded themselves together as the 'Women's Legion' and did sterling work driving cars at all hours of the day and night. Their example was followed by many other women, whose driving skills were greatly valued in the absence of male drivers, and these 'lady drivers' became not only just as skilled as men, but were also accepted and respected on the roads.

Development of motor vehicles did not stand still during the war. Great companies like Rolls-Royce and Daimler, while engaged on producing every type of vehicle and engine for the war effort, were still able to push ahead with research and the development of their engineering skills. In the meantime many from all walks of life were able to see the advantages of motor transport, and to see vehicles operating in challenging and hazardous conditions. Those with a sense of vision could also see the potential for motor vehicles of all types in the future, once peace was restored.

I want to finish this chapter with a puzzle! The photograph above shows my father with his Royal Engineer company. He served on the front line in France throughout the 1914–18 war. Behind the carefully posed company is what appears to be a 30+ foot boat, loaded with materials. The engineers were used to hauling heavy loads about, making bridges and so on, but what could have transported such a large boat overland in 1918? I realise that this could be a photograph taken during training in England as no date is given, or details of location. If anyone can supply further details I should be most interested to receive them. My father, like many soldiers, spoke very little about his war experiences.

Chapter 3

ELEGANCE FOR THE RICH IN THE 1920s

William Merson, owner of Blue Anchor Bay Garage near Carhampton in Somerset, chauffeuring Colonel Gordon of Bicknoller.

This atmospheric photograph, taken in the early 1920s, though the car is a bit older, sums up the situation perfectly. The chauffeur sits upright, looking straight ahead. His passenger, reclining at his ease on the back seat, looks round at the camera. It appears to be on the promenade or beside a river, and on a rather misty day.

It took the world many years to recover from the horror of the war, but the dawn of the 1920s seemed to herald a new age, full of hope, optimism and opportunity. The League of Nations would usher in a period of perpetual peace. Industry and trade would flourish. And travel would become ever easier, thanks to motor transport. Great progress would be seen also in trains, ships and aeroplanes, though the latter had no commercial future, of course!

The motor industry, set free from the constraints of war, had what amounted to a new beginning.

Wartime operations had proved the worth of motor vehicles, and engineering inventions and developments had progressed rapidly. Now was the moment to combine all these things and produce cars the like of which had not even been dreamed of before. In 1920 there were already 21 major car

Blue Anchor Bay Garage, 1933.

When Motoring Was Fun

Unmistakably Rolls-Royce. The 40/50HP new Phantom enclosed-drive limousine. Introduced in 1925, the Phantom took over from the Silver Ghost.

manufacturers in existence in Britain. During the 1920s they were joined by at least 6 more.

All these manufacturers recognised that reliability and comfort were key ingredients to the successful sales of their cars. In particular, those at the expensive end of the market had to justify the prices they asked, and compete with powerful rivals from home and overseas. It was fortunate for them that a number of developments helped a lot. For a start the surfaces of roads was steadily improving, which gave for a smoother ride and fewer punctures, so that the inflatable tyre became an asset rather than a liability.

At this point cars could be divided into three major parts, chassis, engine and body. The chassis not only included much better tyres and wheels, but also better springing, usually with leaf springs but increasingly with independent coil spring suspension in front. Both steering and brakes were much improved during the 20s, which made a big contribution to road safety. Petrol tanks were more robust, and tucked away where they were less likely to be damaged in an accident. Bumpers began to be fitted as standard, to take the impact of any collision.

One of the big problems with the earliest cars had been the level of noise, and steps were taken with the design of engines to see if this noise could be reduced. Engines and other moving parts produce noise in three ways. First moving parts such as gearwheels, fans and flywheels, create noise. Second, the valves and rockers in the engine can be very noisy. Third, the engine exhaust produces high levels of noise. The result was that driver and passengers could not hear themselves speak, and would arrive at their destination partially deaf!

The noise made by moving parts could be muffled somewhat by casings, screens and carpets. The whole bonnet compartment was better insulated to reduce noise, but there were limitations due to the need to have plenty of air circulating around the engine.

Tappets and rockers benefitted from improved design, but the arrival of the Silent Knight sleeve valve engine was a breakthrough. Knight and his invention were American, but he brought the idea to Coventry and offered them to the Daimler Motor Company, who at once saw the merits of the invention and adopted it. A moving sleeve between piston and main cylinder wall operated as a valve, covering and uncovering ports in the outer wall, which acted as valves to the cylinder. This design was not only more efficient and had fewer moving parts, but it was almost completely silent. Silent

Early Days on the Open Road

Grace Creswell standing beside an Austin in Bicknoller, Somerset c.1920.

Knight engines were fitted to other makes as well as Daimlers, and became very popular as a mark of luxury in expensive cars.

Finally, exhaust systems were redesigned on luxury cars, and larger silencers with more baffle plates were fitted. The rear of the exhaust pipe would usually emerge under the back of the car, so that the occupants of the car were less aware of the noise they were making, while those in the car behind got the full benefit! Rolls-Royce would boast that their engines ran so smoothly that you could balance a guinea coin on its edge in the radiator cap and it would stay upright! As the picture opposite shows, the radiator cap on a Rolls was soon adorned with the famous 'Spirit of Ecstasy' figure, so the experiment with the coin became impossible.

The third main component of the car was the body, and here the top makers had varying practices. Daimler tended to build most of their bodies themselves, at Coventry, though later on the larger cars would often have bodies built by other coachbuilders. Rolls-Royce liked to sell a chassis and engine, for about £1200, and then there were a number of coachbuilders like Mulliners, Park Ward, Thrupp and Maperly and Hooper who would build the body. Small companies like the Dorking Motor Company could do the same, investing in a chassis and then building the body almost as a part time hobby. This procedure resulted in a huge number of variations in the design and appearance of these luxury cars, and many prospective owners had their bodies 'made to order'. It was a bit like going to one's bespoke tailor!

Chauffeur Tom Towler with the 1927 Limousine he drove for the Herring Family of Narborough, Norfolk.

When Motoring Was Fun

Daimler was one of the earliest car makers in the field, and attracted the custom of the Royal Family, which was a feather in their cap. For very many years the royal cars were always Daimlers, with specially built bodies to enable the occupants of the car to be seen clearly by people lining the route.

In this period those rich enough to buy and run the most expensive cars would divide into two groups. First there were those for whom the motor car was just a development of the horse-drawn carriage. They would employ a chauffeur instead of a coachman, though many a coachman made the change very efficiently if reluctantly, and the stables would be converted into a garage. They would summon the 'motor' for a certain time, and be driven on whatever errand they required, a visit to a neighbour, or a race meeting, or even some more important shopping perhaps. It is unlikely they would even know the make of their car, unless being able to remind everyone else that it was a Rolls-Royce added much to their sense of self-consequence. The chauffeur was expected to do all the servicing and cleaning necessary, and might every few years advise that getting one of the newer models would be an investment in increased comfort. (He would have to be very tactful about how he broached the subject!).

The other group comprised those who had enjoyed tooling their curricles along challenging roads, or were members of the 'Four in Hand' club of notable whipsters in the days of fine horses. Now they had a new 'steed' to school, and it had great possibilities of speed and excitement. Just as before you could judge a man by the quality of the horse-flesh he drove, so now in the motoring age you could assess him by the make and model of his car, noting any special modifications or extras which had been attached at the drivers command!

There were a large number of companies which produced such thoroughbreds of the road in the 1920s. Bentleys and Lagondas jostled with Bugattis and Hispano-Suizas, Mercedes, and from America Buick and Packard. Every car could be easily distinguished not only by its maker's badge, or special symbol like the 'Spirit of Ecstasy' but also by a distinctive radiator grille or arrangement of lamps and horns. Young boys could recognise a car at a glance, and there would be much excitement if a strange and glamorous car made a first visit to the neighbourhood.

As in former days, some rich men could afford to keep a stable of cars, and took great delight in doing so. As we have seen, motor car races and endurance tests had been well established for over 20 years, and now the fruits of such experience and experiment were to be found in the production cars which anyone could buy if they had the money. The development of the supercharger, for example, by Bentley

The lower end of Fareham High Street in about 1920. On the far left May's Garage, formerly a cycle works, now has a petrol pump for the new motoring age.

Early Days on the Open Road

and Mercedes among others, meant that the enhanced performance was available to everyone. By the end of the 1920s Bentley were producing their fast and famous 4½ litre supercharged car.

It was this car which prompted a famous rival, Mr Ettore Bugatti, to remark 'Mr Bentley makes very fast lorries!' This was a very exciting period for the motorist, for despite General Strikes and looming Depressions, many of the car manufacturers forged ahead with a succession of inspired new models, at very competitive prices. There were a few companies like Marmon in the United States who misread the times and produced a 16 cylinder model at just the wrong moment, to the permanent detriment of their company, but most got it about right, and there were always enough people around with the necessary money to keep the luxury car makers in business. One factor which helped was the limited number of top quality cars produced in a year.

The picture of Fareham High Street (opposite) in about 1920 shows us what a pleasantly traffic-free

age it was, and we may well feel very jealous. One drove on the left, or roughly so, but there were no white or yellow lines, and you parked outside the shop you intended to visit, whichever side of the road it happened to be on! In the photograph two of the three vehicles appear to be facing the wrong way according to present day practice! Bicycles and a handcart are still in evidence, but a lone petrol pump has appeared on the pavement, as a symbol of the changing times. Other pictures from this period also emphasise what a delightfully traffic free era this was!

I could not resist this picture of an elegant Rolls-Royce taking four worried looking occupants up an incredible track. It certainly shows the ability of the 1920s luxury to perform off-road, probably just as well as a 4 x 4 of today! And with a higher degree of comfort, deep leather seats and so on. One remembers that going up was always the easier bit, and what goes up has to come down eventually. One can only hope that the brakes on the Rolls were truly up for the challenge!

An awkward hair-pin near the top of Hard Knott Pass in Lakeland.

Chapter 4

MOTORCYCLES AT WORK AND PLAY

A moped (autocycle) which has been dated by it's registration as c.1913. I would guess it is somewhat later.

The first bicycle appeared in Paris about 1790, and during the 1800s many differing models were developed. It was therefore logical that when a small, light-weight engine became available, attempts should be made to produce a powered bicycle.

At once there was a difference of opinion as to where the engine should be located. Some felt it should be as far away from the rider as possible, perhaps because of possible explosions! On top of the rear wheel was tried, as was a motorised single-wheel trailer connected to the rear of the bicycle. I have a picture of this, but no clear idea as to how the controls for the engine worked, if at all!

At length, for reasons of weight and centre of gravity, as well as controls and transmission, the engine came to be located between the driver's legs, mounted on the lower struts of the frame. From here transmission using a chain or shaft to the rear wheel was quite easy.

The 'transitional' vehicle was the autocycle, which had a small low-powered engine, and retained it's pedals so that the rider could give assistance going up hills. My godmother, Katherine Parker, bought one of these, -very secondhand, in 1940 in South Devon, and rode it east to Portsmouth to join the WRENS. She had never ridden one before as far as I know, so it must have been an exciting voyage!

By 1910 there were many companies making motorcycles, including several like Morris, Brough and BSA which went on to make cars. The motorcycle had several advantages over the car. It was cheaper and quicker to make, required less garage space, had an easily accessible engine, and had good cross country ability. You could pick your way between the potholes on a bad road. Moreover, as we have seen, the motorcycle distinguished itself in the Great War.

The disadvantage of the motorcycle was that it was wet and cold in bad weather, but no more so than some early cars! Also its stability and road holding were not as good as a car, leaving the unprotected rider more at risk.

Early Days on the Open Road

To describe the motorcycle as the 'poor man's car' may sound derogatory, but it was so, and my goodness the poor man enjoyed his machine to the full! The photographs on these pages leave one in no doubt of that at all. Individuals and families for whom travel more than a few miles from their homes had been just a dream suddenly found a huge adventure offered to them.

The motorcycle has always had a huge appeal for young men. It's sensation of speed, noisy exhaust and sensitive response make it irresistible. Further, in about 1930 you were permitted to ride one on the road from the age of fourteen. A motorcycle could be tucked away in a shed, sometimes without the knowledge of parents, and taken out for a spin when enough cash for a gallon of petrol had been saved up. And a motorcycle would go a lot farther on a gallon than a thirsty car.

Owning a motorcycle gave a huge degree of status to a young man, as well as providing the means whereby he would convey his girlfriend well away from home to the seaside, the cinema, or some other excellent courting venue. Thus for many

Dispatch rider Corporal Bromley Penny, MM from Watchet in Somerset, with his machine during the 1914–18 war.

Arthur Jenkins, the village tailor of Sampford Brett, Somerset, sitting proudly on his Raleigh Motorcycle in 1932.

When Motoring Was Fun

Frank Raddy of Looe in Cornwall with his pride and joy in the 1920s.

young couples the motorcycle was the essential member of their ménage-a-trois, and early memories of their relationship often involved incidents of breaking down in unfortunate places or ploughing into an unseen flood in the dark and getting extremely wet!

Many young men learned all the basics of mechanics from looking after their machines, and many a mother was forced into violent remonstration when she returned home from church to cook the Sunday lunch and found a carburettor or gearbox stripped down and displaying many oily bits on the kitchen table!

The simplicity of the motorcycle and its light weight meant that you did not need a garage pit or large quantity of expensive tools to give it the care and attention it deserved.

But it wasn't just the young men. The whole family hankered to get involved, and especially those of the younger generation. It might be considered a bit 'fast' for young ladies in the 1920s to be seen hurtling along on a motorcycle, but for many the machine couldn't go fast enough! As for young boys, as the pictures show they were always looking for an opportunity to 'borrow' dad's or older brother's motorbike!

Incidentally, in the two photographs of members of the Roper family on the family machine, there is a sidecar attached which made it much easier to pose for photographs. These were heavy beasts!

A standard motorcycle was really designed for two adults. Plans to fit a child's seat on the handlebars were looked on with strong disapproval by the authorities, fortunately for the nation's children.

For many families faced with the challenge of 'how many family members can you get on a motorbike' the answer was not to become a circus performing stunt troupe, but to get a sidecar.

The sidecar was well established by the 1920s. Even if it did at times look and feel like a very fast moving coffin, it fulfilled three vital functions for the family. It could accommodate another adult, or

Mollie Roper of Lydford, Devon, and a Roper grandson, trying out the family motorcycle on a quiet stretch of the A386 in the 1930s.

This motorbike and basket sidecar must have been quite a sight in the hamlet of Escalls in Cornwall in the 1920s.

several children. It offered protection, to some degree, against bad weather, though with the roof on many passengers must have been aware of a sense of claustrophobia they had never realised they had suffered from before.

Finally, the sidecar could be used as a cargo carrier, which could be a great advantage to many small businesses.

Sidecars came in all shapes and sizes, and could even be woven like baskets! One feels that the unusual model seen in the photograph above would have been nice and airy in hot summer weather, but very draughty on cold winter days, and ultimately a very tempting feast for an army of woodworm! One wonders whether the body for the sidecar was made by the local basket weaver? Perhaps the original body had come to a sad end.

Meanwhile the sidecar could be adapted for business use, such as transporting a churn full of milk round the village, from which the housewives filled their jugs. The milk was often still warm, and when it cooled had a thick crust of cream on the top. Window-cleaners managed to get ladders on their sidecars long before Wallace & Gromit, and vegetables and poultry could be taken to market. It was advisable for the fowls to be in a box of some sort.

Relatives from London, with capacity for four on their motorcycle combination, visit Fir Cottage, Sampford Courtenay, Devon, in the 1930s.

Milk from the farm at Sennen in Cornwall being taken to the local factory at Bottoms, about 1939.

The passenger helps to turn a hairpin corner at Ramsey, 1930s.

Two riders going up a Lake District mountain in the 1920s.

Sidecars could be detached from the motorcycle fairly easily, which gave a lot of flexibility to the motorcycle combination.

There was one other very exciting use for sidecars, and that was for racing. As can be seen above, the passenger did not have a lot of leisure to enjoy the view!

Looking at recent film footage of the 1950s, we saw a family setting out on their holiday. Their scooter had a smart sidecar attached to it, and was also equipped to pull a substantial camping trailer, full of equipment. One couldn't help feeling that if they were bound for Dartmoor the passengers would find themselves pushing the outfit up hills!

The most famous motorcycle races were the Tourist Trophy races on the Isle of Man, begun in 1907, involve a twisting 37 mile course on public roads. But there were many other courses such as Crystal Palace, Brooklands and Silverstone.

Off-road motorcycling and 'scrambling' have always been very popular. The photograph above shows two riders 'motor mountaineering' in the Lake District. These activities are not at all encouraged in the Lake District now, but show the freedom the motorcycle gave to intrepid individuals in the early days.

Cross country riding could be a daunting and a dampening experience, as can be seen in the next photograph, and the position of the engine did not encourage this sort of adventure. Fortunately someone has organised the course so that the water level is just below the spark plug, but that does not allow for a bow wave. This scene would be late 1920s or early 30s, and probably involved several teams of riders.

John Surtees, one of the greatest ever, in action on a 500cc Augusta.

Taking to the water on a Sunbeam during an inter-varsity trial.

Early Days on the Open Road

Wilfrid Tyler astride his 350cc Ariel.

His and hers, Wilfrid Tyler's rebuilt 16H Norton, and his wife Jill on her ex-parachutists Corgi Minibike.

My oldest brother writes:

In 1946 my first motorcycle was an elderly Francis Barnet 2-stroke. It was a runner, just, but suffered a serious lack of power on a long run. The trouble turned out to be a blocked silencer, caused by the use of ordinary engine oil in the 2-stroke mix of fuel. The solution was to remove the silencer, put a cork in one end and fill it up with a caustic soda solution for 24 hours. You then drained out all the gunge, and magically power was restored, until the next time!

My next purchase was a 350cc Ariel from a local trials rider who ran a motorcycle business in the next village. This machine provided reliable transport for the next two years or so, until I was posted to Egypt in 1949.

Shortly after arriving at my new desert home, I acquired a stripped down ex-army 16H Norton which had been used for a basic form of speedway racing, provided by Army Welfare for the troops. After a number of serious accidents (which didn't contribute to the troops welfare at all) the facility was abandoned and the machines were sold for a modest sum. I set about re-building it to a roadworthy standard, and as we were surrounded by many dumps of

ex-service material from the war, I was able to find all the bits and pieces I needed.

My future wife quickly caught the motorcycle bug, and on a local desert airstrip set off on her first solo ride and quickly disappeared in the distance. At the end of the tarmac was soft sand, and off she came! I was unaware of the pending disaster, as she could not lift the bike back on to the runway.

However, as often happens in the desert, a genie in the shape of a galabia-robed Arab appeared from nowhere, and said 'Elsit (Miss) you are in trouble, I will help you.' In no time the bike was back on the hard stuff, the genie disappeared, and my intended returned safely!'

Motorcycles could be the means of happy social activity, as the story of Dartington Motorcycle Club, in Devon, shows. After the Second World War, young men from the parish returned home and bought motorbikes, because cars were unobtainable or too expensive. Eventually several enthusiasts formed a club, with officers, and with some members coming to join from as far afield as Totnes and Buckfastleigh. Organised runs on a Sunday afternoon became a regular event, with wives, sisters and girlfriends on the pillion seats (woe betide the young man who replaced his sister with a girlfriend, it was a good idea to look for a sidecar very quickly!). Sometimes four or five bikers participated, sometimes a dozen or more. Riders would meet at Cott Cross, Dartington, and then perhaps go up on to Dartmoor, with it's stimulating breezes,

When Motoring Was Fun

Members of the Dartington Motorcycle Club, Devon, on Dartmoor in 1949.

Left: *Members of the Dartington Motorcycle Club at Slapton Sands, South Devon, in the later 1940s.*

Below left: *Edgar Hodge, Dartington Motorcycle Club Treasurer, on his trusty AJS, late 1940s.*

or down to the South Devon Coast. They might even take the Saltash Ferry and venture into deepest Cornwall.

The club flourished for several years, with members taking part in local scrambling trials, but when petrol rationing was re-introduced in the mid-1950s

as a result of the Suez crisis, the club had to be disbanded. It was no fun pushing motorcycles that had run out of coupons up Devon hills! Sadly the club was never re-formed, but by that time many of the young men needed family transport!

During the sixty years from 1890 to 1950, design of motorcycles meant huge improvements, and the performance of the machines became more and more impressive.

Frames and springing were made much stronger, and springs ensured a much more comfortable ride. Almost all makers opted for chain drive from the gearbox to the rear wheel, but a few luxury machines had a shaft drive instead. The main changes were seen in engine design, with single cylinder, V-twin, and two- or four-cylinder horizontally opposed engines. Engines could also be water cooled or air cooled, the latter being the most usual because of its simplicity.

The improvement in engine performance meant ever faster top speeds, and better and better fuel consumption, which has always been a very desirable feature of the motorbike, especially as fuel prices always seem to be going up! To cope with the speeds, brakes had to be greatly improved, and the riders protected as much as possible. My book from the 1930s rather bemoans the need for racing en-

Early Days on the Open Road

thusiasts to wear crash helmets, but then reflects that top hats are worn in the hunting field, and have saved many a skull from damage, so it is really quite a good idea! But in every motorcycle picture from the 20s to the 50s there is not a crash helmet to be seen.

Down the years the motorcycle has always retained its great attraction. Cheaper, lighter, easy to garage, abstemious drinker. Further, as we have seen, it can go places other larger vehicles cannot go, and still does. Another advantage has become ever more apparent as our roads increase in congestion, and that is the ability of the motorbike to squeeze through when everyone else is enjoying a total traffic jam! Car owners are not always happy about this, but that is only because they are jealous!

Then, just when some people were predicting that the motorbike had had it's day, along came the scooter.

The scooter, by its clean and uncomplicated design, proved ideal for both sexes to go shopping round town or far a spin in the country, and again scooter clubs flourished. It was not as heavy or noisy as the motorbike, and did not go so fast, so daughters were permitted to ride them!

'Off to the Sea', a BSA advertising jig-saw puzzle from the 1930s, and not a crash helmet in sight!

The picture above, by an unknown artist but surely done as an advertising poster, sums it all up. Powerful gleaming motorcycles, their young happy riders casually dressed and with streaming scarves, what a contrast to leathers and crash helmets. And a perfect day by the sea, with unbroken sunshine! And if it had rained, they would sensibly have stayed at home!

The author (left) and brother on oldest brother's motorcycle, the Francis Barnet 2-stroke.

The motorcycle provided the stepping stone from bicycle to car for thousands of young people during the period we have been considering, but it was far more than that. It was truly 'A Transport of Delight' and the witness to that are all the older people who have continued to ride motorcycles from choice down the following years.

Charlie Copp on a scooter, with friends outside the Old Post Office, Willand, Somerset, in the 1950s.

Chapter 5

A CHUMMY FAMILY

Ern Barkell sitting proudly in his Model T Ford, one of the first cars in Bridestowe, Devon, c.1920.

In the early years of the twentieth century there were a number of motor car pioneers on both sides of the Atlantic who had engineering ability and foresight. These men saw what the motor car could become in the future, and set out to make it happen. I am going to chose two, but they represent all the others.

Henry Ford and others set up the Ford Motor Company in Detroit, USA in 1903. Their first car was the Model A, and in due course their greatest success was the Model T, of which fifteen million cars were built between 1908 and 1927, and which 'put America on wheels.'

Ford demanded three things of his Model T. It must be simple, it must be rugged, and above all it must be cheap. The USA was and is a vast, spacious country, with many remote areas. Ford's car must be strong and easy to maintain far away from sophisticated workshops. It must be able to travel roads hardly worthy of the name.

To achieve a cheap car Ford pioneered mass production, with an assembly line and as much standardisation as possible. He even standardised the colour, you could have your car any colour you liked, he said, as long as it was black! This not only simplified production, but also the supply of spare parts, which would always fit your car.

England is not such a spacious country as the USA, and has many winding lanes and narrow village and town streets. Herbert Austin wanted to build a small, strong, cheap family car. He was chief designer for Wolseley Cars up to 1905, when he left to found his own company. He had only £5000 capital, and had to be content with buying a disused canning factory at Longbridge, south of Birmingham, and equipping it for car production.

The design of the first Austin car was shown at the London Fair in November 1905, with an announcement that the first cars would be delivered in March 1906 and would cost £650.

This car was the 15/20hp model, and it duly appeared in April 1906, showing that Austin could deliver as promised.

In 1909 Herbert Austin gave a preview of his vision of the future when he brought out the first Austin 7. This car was updated in 1911, and is seen to be a very smart little tourer, seating two people. It had good leaf springs, mudguards and running boards, but was singularly lacking in the headlight department. Perhaps it wisely did not venture out

A very smart Austin Chummy of the 1920s, pretending to be a Rolls-Royce!

at night. It did however have an efficient manually operated horn, sited within easy reach of the driver's right hand, and able to make a wandering pedestrian jump in a very satisfactory manner!

There was another difference between England and the USA. From 1914 to 1918 England was heavily involved in a life-and-death struggle in France, while the US. only joined the fray in the last year of the war. England emerged exhausted, her manpower decimated and her industries in a sad way. It was not until 1922 that Herbert Austin was able to bring out his improved Austin 7, and meanwhile Henry Ford had produced millions of his Model T's in the States.

In the 1920s the Austin 7 Chummy, as it was christened, became ever more popular. For many families keeping a horse and coach, or even a pony and trap had been just a dream. Even a donkey cart required space.

Then there was the cost involved, and the need for some sort of stable, not to mention winter forage. Many families had to rely on their legs, and to hope that the nearest railway station or bus/tram route was not too far away.

The little Chummy could be garaged in a garden shed if need be, and many semi-detached houses in the 1920s had just enough space between each pair of houses for the car to squeeze through. Once in its little garage it could be cherished and polished, and protected from the cold winter weather with rugs and a radiator muff. It would be lovingly

An Austin Chummy in West Street, Watchet, in the 1920s.

cleaned and polished once a week, and then brought out into the street in very good time for the proposed journey so that all the neighbours could admire it.

Herbert Austin was determined that his baby car would be in truth a large car in miniature, and he largely achieved this. There had been baby cars before, as the photograph overleaf shows, but they had often had unreliable 2-stroke engines, driving through belts which often broke, and because the engines were often air cooled they had a tendency to run red hot which could be most uncomfortable. In fact the 'baby' car did not have a good reputation.

A particularly unusual baby three-wheeler of 1907 vintage, said to be a Quadrant 7hp Tri-car.

The car above is a Quadrant 7 horsepower Tri-car, originally manufactured in 1907. It was a tricycle design, with the engine mounted between the front wheels. The car was much modified over the next few years, and this is probably a homemade body. It does boast a splendid horn and impressive lamps, but the windscreen is a bit deficient!

Herbert Austin's baby car, which he produced just in time to save his company from bankruptcy in 1922, was a masterpiece of design. The chassis was an A- frame shape, with the engine mounted at the pointed end on a sub-frame. At the rear leaf springs projected from the end of the chassis to support the rear axle.

The early cars were all tourers, with bucket seats at the front, and a bench at the back for children, livestock or other cargo. Some said the little cars were called 'Chummies' because the occupants had to be on very good terms with one another if they were to enjoy a journey squashed into a body about three feet square!

The Austin 7 also had its peculiar challenges. The general ride was skittish, and the steering was decidedly vague and loose, so that the little car had a strong tendency to wander across the road and back. The experience of being overtaken on a dual carriageway by a modern juggernaut was so terrifying as to turn hair white on the spot. One was scooped up and had no idea whether you would end up under the juggernaut or roll down the left hand side and end up in the ditch.

Finally, and most alarmingly, there was the brakes. It is true that few cars in 1922 had four-wheel braking, and this was fitted to comply with the new law that all cars were to have two independent sets of brakes. But most cars could stop a lot quicker than the Austin 7 with rear brakes only. The rear brake drums were so small and inefficient that they were next to useless, and the front brakes were operated by cables which pulled on the diagonal, and tended to pull the brake levers outwards, instead of backwards.

The result really was very frightening but Herbert Austin countered criticism by asserting that good brakes only encouraged bad driving! I was very tempted to carry a length of rope attached to an anchor when I drove my own Austin 7, and by that time the brakes were a good deal better!

Having virtually no brakes, the driver had to rely heavily on his engine to diminish his speed as well as accelerate. The little 747cc engine was very game, but again there was a challenge for the driver in the clutch and gearbox department. First, the clutch had a total travel of about a quarter of an inch between engaged and fully disengaged. This meant that many an Austin 7 in the hands of a less than totally skilled driver progressed like a kangaroo much of the time, and especially when starting from rest.

The three- and later four-speed gearbox contained some very curious ratios, but luckily first gear was designed to enable the car to tow a caravan up Porlock Hill, and so it was hard to stall the engine even when one's control of the clutch was rudimentary. In fact you could put the car into bottom gear, let in the clutch, and get out of the car, and it would toddle along at walking pace with the engine just ticking over. I have done it!

Gears were selected with a long floppy gear lever. Getting from one gear position to the next involved some guesswork and a good deal of luck. Doing the

Delilah, my Austin 7 Box Saloon of 1933 vintage, dressed for a wedding.

change from third to second, to slow descent on a steep hill, with the necessary double de-clutching involved, was the sort of manoeuvre which deserved a medal if done without too much noise or bad language!

Throughout the 1920s Austins continued to develop their baby car, and then in 1931 came a big change. The wheelbase was lengthened to make the car a full four-seater, though it helped a lot if the rear seat passengers were on the small side! The cost of the car was between £118 and £128, competing well with the new Morris Minor which cost £100 but had a fabric body.

I first set eyes on my Austin 7 at a wet Country Sports Day. She was last in line of a row of pseudo-vintage cars, and looked rather sad and bedraggled. A notice on the windscreen declared that she was for sale, and gave a phone number. I stopped for a closer look, and my escorting daughter said 'Come on dad, its not a Dinky Toy, and anyway you're too fat to get into it.' I deliberately stopped longer, and wrote down the phone number! I had no intention of buying the car, but I did phone up to ask how much the owner wanted for it. He had been posted suddenly on business to the Middle East, and his wife was desperate to sell the car. Feeling that I must

encourage her, I made an offer I knew she would not accept, and after consulting with her husband, she did! I drove Delilah home (so named because she had tempted me) and quickly discovered a lot of the interesting features of an Austin 7 which I have already mentioned!

Delilah was a delight, great fun to drive, and almost trouble free. On the only occasion I had a problem with a sheered bracket on the top radiator hose I took her to my local garage, and Jeff looked at it and recommended I go across the road to the blacksmith. Mr Miles, always a helpful friend, did a perfect repair that took five minutes, and cost me fifty pence. That was very good value, even in the 1980s. We used to run a youth club, and on several occasions the young people took turns to drive Delilah round our front lawn when it was dry. In bottom gear they could come to no harm, and several dozen were able to claim that the first car they ever drove was an Austin 7.

We had many happy hours motoring in Delilah, but one day we were pottering along a small road when I found myself being overtaken by an entire funeral procession. The undertaker, an old friend, gave me a cheerful wave as he went by, but the mourners looked decidedly un-amused. It was at that point that my wife made an almost unheard of remark from wives, 'I think we shall have to get a car that goes a bit faster!'

My first car, Lucy, a Morris 8 Tourer built in 1935, and lovely on a sunny day.

The early 1930s saw a flourishing of small family cars in England, in the 7–10 horsepower range. Austin, as we have seen, redesigned their 7, and soon introduced the bigger 10. Morris attempted to undercut the market with their £100 Morris Minor, which became the Series 1 Morris 8. This was an attractive car, especially in the tourer form, and it was a comfortable 4-seater. It had a side-valve engine of 918cc, and a three-speed gearbox, which coped with the Devon hills quite courageously.

My oldest sister had the Morris 8 saloon, and I remember a memorable journey from Salisbury to Winchester, with three of us on board. The road across that part of Salisbury Plain is a switchback, and the little car struggled manfully up the hills, and then when the summit was reached my sister kept her foot hard down on the accelerator, and we hurtled down the other side.

At about 38mph everything on the little car vibrated violently, as though we were going through the sound barrier, but at 41mph it all became totally peaceful again, apart from engine and road noise!

Over 20 years of design progress on the Austin 7. My older brother's and sister's cars, Elm Park, Devon about 1957.

In 1932 Ford decided that there might be money to be made with small cars, and showed a prototype in February of that year which bore a strong resemblance to the latest Austin 7. However the first model 8 production saloon, produced later that year, looked very different, and had a 4-speed synchromesh gearbox which was a first in the field, and put down a marker for its competitors.

In the 1930s it has to be said that Ford had a bit of a reputation for being 'cheap and cheerful' Their engines were good, but bodywork was rather thrown together, after all they only cost £100!

The story goes that one eager new owner went to his Ford garage and paid over his money. He was just about to leave, clutching his logbook and receipt, when the salesman dashed back into the office and returned carrying a squirrel in a cage.

'This goes with the new car, sir,' he said.

'What do you mean, goes with the car?' asked the new owner.

'It's all part of the package, sir' said the salesman, proffering the cage with enthusiasm.

'Why would I want a squirrel?' asked the perplexed new owner.

'It's specially trained to run behind the car and pick up the nuts!'

One of the companies who were earliest in the field with their baby car was Jowett. They were always pioneers in the design of cars, and favoured the horizontally opposed cylinder design. The Jowett 7 was produced also in the early 1920s, with a twin

Sergeant Philip Wilks and Joe with a Ford 8 Y Model at Narborough House in 1940.

Early Days on the Open Road

Ted Stooke of Rattery with his Model Y Ford 8 saloon in the 1930s.

cylinder engine which gave a very economical performance. Further the little car was a comfortable 4-seater, at a very competitive price. It sold very well, even if it could not compete with the Austin 7.

It is not possible to mention all the companies that produced the smaller family cars, especially those on the continent like Renault and Fiat. Some, like Clyno, produced relatively few cars.

The Hillman Company, founded by William Hillman, a famous motorist of the early twentieth century, produced their first 9hp car in 1912, and always realised the value of small cars. In 1931 the

May Harvey, postmistress of Widicombe, with her new Austin car about 1930.

first Hillman Minx was produced, and this proved to be a very successful model, being developed and upgraded through the 1930s.

A 1939 Hillman Minx was probably the first car I ever travelled in, my father having bought it in that year. It was an amazing little car, serving a family of 2 adults and 9 children, plus dog, and doing well over 200 000 miles of Devon driving. It did have a few adventures, like taking a huge family party to my grandmother's memorial service in a remote Cornish village on Bodmin Moor, and while crawling up a particularly steep hill breaking a half shaft. The brakes wouldn't hold the car, but my father managed to get it up against the hedge without doing too much damage, and we all piled out very quickly. We had to be rescued by a taxi from the next door village to home, in Devon, and drove back in style. My poor father had to go back by train to recover the car once it had been repaired.

My father bought this car new from Harrison's Garage in Totnes for £185. When he was finally able to replace it in 1952 it was immediately sold to a honeymoon couple for £425, who drove it off in delight. My father always said his mistake was not to have bought half a dozen of them!

The 1939 Minx had an 1184cc side valve engine, the same engine I have in my present car, and in

Our faithful Hillman Minx on Dartmoor, with some of the occupants enjoying the fresh air, c.1950.

that year one of them won its class in the Monte Carlo Rally. However our family car never had much chance to show its paces, being usually loaded down to the gunwales, and clambering up a Devon hill. Two other companies which should be mentioned are Singer and Standard. Both produced small family cars in the 1930s, and the Singer 9 came as a very sporty open car which won a lot of competitions.

Ford summed up the change in motoring and car ownership which took place in the 1930s with one of their posters. It shows a family in their Ford 8 Model Y, gleaming and new, cruising down the road, dad at the wheel with mum beside him, and two children in the back.

In the foreground is a bus stop, where dad and mum, and their two children are waiting for a bus. The young boy is pointing wistfully at the shining Ford going by in style. The caption is 'It can be yours, the £100 Ford Saloon.'

Now, of course, we are all bidden to leave our cars in the garage and wait at the bus stop!

In spite of the fact that Honiton High Street is a little more congested these days than it was in 1926, even with the bypass, I can testify from personal experience to the huge difference having a car made to us as a family, though we used buses, trains, bicycles and even sledges when occasion dictated it. Living 6 miles from the nearest town, the little Hillman was our lifeline.

Following the Second World War, and the continuing rationing of fuel, small cars continued to be in great demand. All the companies mentioned revised their models, and Austin, with the A30, and Morris with the Minor, set new and exciting standards for small cars.

Ford betrayed their American roots once they had finished with the 'sit up and beg' Ford Popular. The Popular derived from the new Ford 8 of 1937, and looked very much the pre-war car it was. It was a very sturdy car, with plenty of power, and it served Ford very well until superseded by the more American looking Popular in the mid 1950s. It was

Honiton High Street, Devon, about 1926, with lots of cars and motorcycles in evidence.

Enjoying open top motoring at Zeal Farm, Bampton in the 1930s. It looks like a Trojan?

A very smart Ford Popular, flanked by two scooters, provides complete family transport for a Llangain family, in Wales c.1960.

powered by a side-valve engine of 1172 cc which Ford put into their three small cars, the Popular, Anglia and Prefect.

There was always a tendency for a car manufacturer to come up with an excellent idea, say the Austin 7 Chummy, and then to feel the public demanded improvements year by year, so that it evolved into the Box Saloon, and then became the Ruby, and finally in 1939 was marketed as the Big Seven Forlite Saloon. It was now a larger and much more sophisticated car, and the owner of a 1922 Chummy would not have recognised it as an Austin 7 at all.

Finally, in the 1950s the car makers decided that the small family car should be gently superseded. True, the Morris Minor, Austin A30 and small Fords enjoyed great popularity, but the long-running Hillman Minx became a bigger car, and in general the family was encouraged to aim for greater size, speed and comfort. The overhead valve engine was fitted as standard in almost every car, and this gave much improved performance in terms of both speed and fuel economy. Once the scare of the Suez crisis and the consequent petrol rationing was over, everyone took to the road with enthusiasm, with Mr Macmillan's words 'You've never had it so good' ringing in our ears!

But where to go from here? A few companies, like Volkswagen and Morgan refused to make more than a token concession to the call for constant change. Ford, Vauxhall and others upgraded the family car so that Cortinas and Escorts were the main diet for their customers. These certainly proved to be roomy, comfortable, speedy machines, and many a family, including my own, enjoyed them.

It took a single designer, Alec Issigonis, to come up with a brilliant new idea, and it was the rather overlarge British Leyland, the product of the merger of Austin and Morris, which put it into production. The Austin 7/Morris Mini-Minor appeared in 1959, and swept the board. There is the story of a small flock of them doing a test run on the newly opened M1 motorway, and considerably startling other motorists as they shot up the motorway at the maximum permitted speed, rather like a flock of partridges with the wind behind them!

The secret of the Mini design was the exact reverse of the long established Volkswagen. Porsche had put his flat-four engine, gearbox and drive at the back of the car. Issigonis, relying on improved design experience, put a transverse engine in the front, with all the gearbox and transmission beneath it, driving onto the front wheels.

He then put a wheel at each corner, rather like the design of the original Chummy, but the wheels were a lot smaller, and so he made available for passenger accommodation the vast proportion of his small car. This proved to be a comfortable 4-seater, with a remarkable performance. The hotted-up Mini Cooper won the prestigious Alpine Rally in 1963, which was a real feather in Issigonis's cap.

The result of the runaway success of the Mini was that the other makers were forced to follow, and produce new 'baby' cars of their own. But the Fiesta and Nova, and others, never really competed with the exciting design of the Mini, or came near to equalling its remarkable performance. The new larger version does not seem to have quite the same appeal. In the picture on the following page the mini looks as though it would fit easily inside the van on the right!

This view of Fore Street, Seaton, Devon, in about 1962, shows a clear contrast between the size of a Mini, parked, and the passing Ford Eight. Below: Somerset District Nurses Jinny Nash and Pat Stowell at Watchet in 1965 with their indispensible Mini saloon.

As with the original Austin 7, and the later A30, the small Austins provided essential transport for many professional people, including District Nurses. As a District Nurse had to carry an increasing amount of equipment around her district, and areas became bigger, she could no longer manage on a bicycle as in former days, and the A30 became a much used District Nurse car, together with the Morris Minor. The coming of the Mini provided an even better vehicle, easy to park in congested streets and manoeuvre through narrow country gateways, but able to carry 4 passengers or a substantial load.

Chapter 6

TRANSPORTS OF DELIGHT ON HOLIDAY

My father took his new wife Rosia on a touring honeymoon in the Lake District, c.1927, in a Morris Cowley.

We have seen how prior to the First World War the motor car was really the preserve of the richer members of society, and how this gradually changed through the 1920s and 1930s in spite of the depression. By 1939 many families had a car, often very second hand, and lovingly maintained by the master of the house with the aid of all sorts of pieces of wire and tape.

In the 1920s the widespread use of motor transport gave the average family the opportunity to travel, and in particular go on holiday. In another chapter we shall look at the part played by buses and charabancs, but the car was also a most important part in this whole social change. A family could be quite easily loaded into a car, and could drive away to the moors or the seaside for a holiday. Trains had already led to the development of many beautiful seaside resorts, like Bournemouth and Scarborough, and Britain offered unparalleled beauty and scenery in a relatively small space. Added to this, unless you wanted to drive to the top of Ben Nevis as one party did, the roads were surprisingly good by the end of the 1920s.

Further, in Britain everything seemed to be in miniature compared with the United States, for example. Places to eat, sleep and fill up your car with petrol were to be found at regular intervals even in quite remote areas. Petrol was cheap, and accommodation at a village inn or bed and breakfast farm was very reasonable. Above all, for many families there was a real sense of adventure, the feeling that the horizon had suddenly been pushed much further away, and they could visit places they had only read about in books or magazines.

Then there was the touring holiday, or even a honeymoon. As seen in the photograph, my father took his new bride on a touring honeymoon in the Lake District. You cruised along by day, enjoying the scenery and perhaps having a picnic at lunch time wherever you happened to find yourselves, and then in the late afternoon you found a nice place to stay, and settled in for the night with a welcome cup of tea and the promise of a delicious meal to come. The secret to this type of holiday was the fact that the roads were so empty that the actual driving was a pleasure and excitement as well.

Sadly as more and more vehicles appeared on the roads, and it became very advisable always to book accommodation well in advance, so the touring holiday became a pleasure of the past.

When Motoring Was Fun

The Blease Family from Staverton in Wiltshire enjoy an outing to the countryside in their Model T Ford in the 1920s.

By 1920, with the recent experience of the War, there would still have been many adults and children in Britain who had never seen the sea.

A visit to the seaside was always a great attraction, as well as supposedly being very beneficial for one's health, and an opportunity to purchase some really fresh fish from a local fisherman. Seaside communities were not slow to realise the benefits to their income that such trippers would bring, and they proceeded to establish car parks, cafes, and other suitable facilities for the benefit of their visitors.

The car park at Sennen Cove, seen in the photograph right, was established by the owner of the land, Mr Barton, as early as the 1920s. As we can see, by the 1940s when this picture was taken, it is pretty well full, with a mixture of pre- and post-war cars. I don't know what the fee for a days parking was.

In 1936 the grain clipper *Herzogen Cecile* ran aground on the rocks just west of Bolt Head on the South Devon coast, and this disaster was announced on the early morning radio news. It was a Sunday, and promised to be a fine and warm April day, with the early morning fog, which had been the ships downfall, soon lifting. From all over the South West of England people climbed into their

The car park, established at Sennen Cove in the 1920s, is seen here in the later 1940s.

cars and headed for the site of the shipwreck. The lanes for miles around became totally jammed with cars, but the quick thinking farmer who owned the clifftop land where the ship lay at once opened up several of his fields as car parks, and charged a shilling a time for car parking. It is said he earned enough in a week to retire on in great comfort!

One of the popular places to visit was a local inn, especially one which had an excellent reputation for its beer. This was no new idea, of course, and in the days of the horse many a steady or unsteady drinker was assisted on to the back of his horse, and the animal, having received a hearty pat on the rump, would unerringly convey its master safely home.

Early Days on the Open Road

The Fox Inn at Midford, Somerset, in 1913, with a large party. Did they all manage to get into the car?

Lustleigh Green in the late 1930s, and it is most obvious that the photographer is more interested in Joy Kitson on her horse, than the Vauxhall behind her!

Here, however, the horse is still one up on the new fangled car, for even our present day computerised cars are not capable of being so helpful, and you would be justly breathalysed into the bargain!

The arrival of the car gave a boost to some meetings involving horses. People could go more easily to the Meet of their local hunt, and some even became very expert at following hounds in their motor car, a form of the sport much frowned upon by those on horseback.

Early in the Second World War a photograph was taken at a race meeting, showing a lot of well off spectators who had driven over to attend the meeting in their cars. Race meetings were certainly much better patronised since the arrival of the car, but this did not accord at all with wartime petrol rationing, and the slogan 'No Motoring for Pleasure' became a war cry for all non-motorists.

In the case of our family, we were a little more fortunate than most because my father commanded quite a large area in the Home Guard, and my mother was very involved in the Girl Guide movement. Both I think were issued with a small extra ration of petrol. Sometimes, when my parents were on 'official business' one or two members of the family stowed away in the family car, but most of the time it was bicycles.

Those who were involved in commercially important activities, or vital war work, like farmers, received an extra allowance of petrol, but this had a special red dye in the fuel, and was known as 'pink petrol'. You were in really serious trouble if you

My father took this photograph of his parents posing in front of his 1934 Hillman 14 Tourer.

were found with pink petrol in the tank of your car. There was a rumour that if you strained the pink petrol through your gas mask you could strain out the dreaded dye, but I have never met anyone who had tried it, and I rather think it was a leg pull. At any rate it would not have done your gas mask a lot of good!

The photographs on the previous page capture something of the happy motoring days of the 1930s. My father bought the Hillman 14 Tourer when he returned to this country from Kenya, and it proved an ideal family car, rugged and spacious. Unfortunately, it also drank rather a lot, so soon after the outbreak of war it was 'laid up' in one half of the garage and became a marvellous play facility for those of us children big enough to clamber on to the running board and open a door. In our imaginations we travelled many miles at the wheel of that trusty car.

As the war progressed, it became a useful storage space for items no longer wanted, or awaiting repair. I remember two of the dining room chairs in that latter category. After the war finished the moment came to clear out and extract the old car, now up for sale, and we found that on our wonderful journeys we had been accompanied by a large contingent of rats. The rat hunt which followed is one of the high points of my childhood!

In 1939, my father set out to fulfil a lifetime's ambition, and wrote to order a new Rover 16 saloon. He received a letter back saying his name was on the waiting list, but delivery would take a few months. In September he received another letter saying that due to the noisy and tiresome activities of a nasty little ex-corporal in Berlin all car production had ceased, and Rover had to concentrate solely on armoured cars.

Finally, in 1952, my father got another letter from Rover saying they were sorry that all cars were still for export, but if he could demonstrate that he was a farmer, he could purchase one of the new Land Rovers.

My father responded by return. He had orchards, a paddock, and nine children as livestock. Surely he was truly a farmer?

Rover seemed to agree, and our wonderful new Land Rover duly arrived. My father fitted it with special side-facing seats in the rear, so that it could carry about 12 people if several were children.

The next year, 1953, was the Coronation, and my mother decided that a large party should go up to London to see all the celebrations. This we duly did, and watched from a shop in Regent Street. My father, wisely, took the two youngest children to an almost deserted London Zoo.

My most vivid memory of the trip was the occasion mother drove her full Land Rover up Knightsbridge at some speed, and swung into the circuit at Hyde Park Corner. I have never, before or since, seen London Taxis scatter like a flock of fowls. By their behaviour you would have thought my Mother was Boadicea and had got long knives on the Land Rover wheels. The Land Rover proved to be an ideal family chariot!

The scene at Widecombe Fair in 1936. Already traffic and parking are becoming a problem, a true foretaste of what is to come.

Early Days on the Open Road

The Angela Caravan Works at Friars Wash, Markyate, Herts, in about 1931.

An early caravan on tour in the later 1920s, somewhere in England!

The photograph of Widecombe Fair is interesting as it shows a very early ice cream van parked on the left, with a young lady being served with what would have been a very creamy ice cream in the heart of Devon in the 1930s.

The snail is beautifully designed to carry its house upon its back, and there are several similarities to one special transport of delight, the caravan. This home on wheels can be towed wherever one wishes to go, and is then ready to provide all home comforts in a few minutes. It was unfortunate that due to switchback and narrow country roads, and the towing vehicle usually being a Standard 10 or Vauxhall Viva, the caravan had another similarity to the snail, its speed on the road!

Also, while there have always been those whose management of a caravan was expert in every way, there were also people who thought you just hooked it on to the back of your car and off you go. The problems of 'snaking' when going downhill could catch them out with devastating results, and when it came to reversing the caravan they were hopeless. I confess I have only once towed a caravan, using a moderately suitable car, and the week's experience taught me a lot. The caravan in

question had not been out before that year, and we found ourselves sharing the bed with a very sleepy queen wasp. Luckily I was a little less sleepy than the wasp, and got my swot in first.

The caravan was first developed in the 1920s, though there were homemade attempts before that. It was of course inspired by the traditional gipsy caravan, and the influence can clearly be seen in the earlier examples. In the 1920s and 30s caravans became larger, partly to provide more accommodation, and partly to take advantage of the much increased power of many family cars. The fitting out of the caravans was done with great care and skill, making the interiors most attractive and provided with many homely touches such as cleverly concealed mirrors and tables. Fragile items were also carefully secured to prevent damage.

A beautifully restored 1930s caravan, with its matching Austin Saloon towing car.

The other way of taking your own house on holiday meant piling several tents on to the car roof rack, or into a trailer. This again gave happy campers a lot of freedom, especially as most farmers were kind and helpful, but it was always essential to carry a spade, and a container for transporting water over long distances!

A new caravan outside the Angela Works, Markyate, waiting for a new owner in 1931.

When Motoring Was Fun

Looking back, we shamefully abused the poor car, loading it up with a family of six, boats, full camping gear and a large dog!

The original Caravan Club was founded as long ago as 1907, but the vans were horse-drawn, and it was not until about 1915 that the first motor car drawn caravan arrived.

Since the Second World War, and with much better roads and more powerful cars, towing a caravan has become easier and safer, in spite of problems with drivers who seem to forget they have a van behind when putting their foot on the accelerator!

Today the Caravan Club flourishes, and has access to hundreds of beautiful sites all round the country. It organises frequent rallies which are well attended by its enthusiastic members.

One other factor that makes a camping or caravan holiday very attractive, once you have bought your tent or caravan, is the cost. It can be a very cheap holiday, even if it is not much of a holiday for mum, required to produce first class meals and deprived of most of her domestic appliances at home.

Another factor is the freedom, you can get up when you like, go to bed when you like, have meals when you like, and no landlady or hotel porter will inspect your shoes for unwanted sand when you return to your accommodation. But if it should rain for days on end, then it is rather a different story!

By the 1930s the ordinary motorist could venture quite far afield with confidence, and in 1936 my mother and several lady friends drove a Morris Cowley to Austria, where they stayed in a little village in the Tyrol. My mother never divulged any details of this memorable trip, but it left her with a strong desire to go back to Pettneu, and a determination not to endure another sea crossing of the English Channel.

In 1954 we had the Land Rover as our family vehicle, and mother discovered that it was possible to fly the channel with Silver City Airways. Accordingly the expedition was scheduled for the summer holidays, and my father fitted a large cabin trunk on the tailgate, secured with ropes. Finally we were ready to go, and my father stood at the gate to see us off, alternately waving and weeping into a large white handkerchief. Then he went indoors to enjoy five weeks of perfect peace with the dogs. My father was a very wise man!

We flew the channel from Lympne, in Kent, and I don't think the Bristol Freighter aircraft had ever swallowed a Land Rover before. It managed it with inches to spare. There were eighteen passengers in the cramped little cabin, and the plane bounced

Ladies enjoying a leisurely afternoon with the radio outside the caravan, with spacious awnings, and Bull Nose Morris in the New Forest in the 1930s.

Early Days on the Open Road

The Land Rover fully loaded, and with the help of a Bristol Freighter aircraft we arrive in Austria, 1954.

down the grass runway with much noise and vibration. I am sure it was all quite safe, but roaring along apparently a couple of hundred feet above the waves it seemed a bit hairy. We were very relieved to be on the ground at Le Touquet.

The journey to Austria was without incident, and the Land Rover excited a lot of interest. We even helped with the hay harvest on a farm in Pettneu, pulling the farmer's trailer. I shall refer to other features of the trip later!

Many other motorists conquered their fears over cross Channel ferries, if they had any, and an increasing torrent of cars made their way across the Channel every year, to many European countries. Ports like Dover, Newhaven and Southampton developed large ferry terminals where hundreds of cars a day could be trans-shipped. Even the Isle of Wight and many Scottish Islands benefitted from improved ferries, and motorists could explore ever more remote locations.

There was, of course, one small challenge about Continental motoring, and that was that our European friends persisted in driving on the wrong side of the road! Oh yes, and one other slight problem. Not every foreigner could speak and understand English, even if we spoke slowly and raised our voices a little!

In far more distant and remote countries the motor car was having a huge impact, and a vehicle like the Model T Ford, because of its good ground clearance and rugged construction was ideal.

My father worked in Kenya from 1919 to 1934, and I believe he was one of the first settlers to import motor vehicles for his forestry and farming business in the early 1920s. He had seen the value of such vehicles up to 1914 in England, and even more during the First World War in France.

In a 'frontier' country like Kenya, the horse was still the go-anywhere means of transport, but could not carry heavy loads, so my father imported Chevrolet lorries to carry the timber from the forest to the railway station. These lorries had a special

A Model T Ford equipped as safari vehicle encounters a rather deep river in Kenya in about 1924.

When Motoring Was Fun

My father's Model T Ford on Safari in Kenya c.1925.

The Crossley Tourer with a full load of family, Molo, Kenya, c.1932.

differential which could be locked to give twice the traction in a sticky situation. As can be seen in the photographs, the Model T Ford was his ideal safari wagon, and he also used it when he went to look for gold. The vehicle was excellent, but the gold proved to be non-existent!

My father would return to England almost every year, in spite of it being a tedious journey by train and ship, and often used the visit to buy a new vehicle. One year he gave himself a treat, and bought a Crossley Tourer. It travelled out as deck cargo on the ship with him, and his plan was to drive it up to Nairobi from Mombasa, and on to his home in Molo. He supervised the unloading at the

dock, and then set off on his journey. It soon became apparent that the car was very unwell, with sluggish performance and no power to climb hills. At length my father accepted the inevitable, stopped at the roadside, and began to inspect the engine. There was no visible problem, but he took the cap off the distributor and looked at the points. On the long sea voyage the salt air had caused a layer of mould to form. A quick rub with a piece of emery paper, and my father found he was driving a completely different car!

As well as being the ideal safari vehicle in Africa, specially adapted vehicles were used for every kind of cross country challenge. Expeditions tackled the Sahara Desert, usually with tracks fitted to the rear wheels, and additional wheels to cope with the soft sand. The photograph of the half-track Citroen on page 119 shows the type of vehicle used.

Others travelled from Cairo to the Cape of Good Hope, and crossed Asia. Some of the old photographs make you wonder how the vehicles survived at all. In the year 1924 Major Court Treatt did the journey from Cape Town to Cairo, facing many hazards. Mud was his favourite problem, of which there was an abundance.

All over the world the coming of the motor car revolutionised the holidays of millions of people, and led to a new spirit of enquiry and adventure for very many individuals and families.

Chapter 7

RELUCTANT STARTERS, BREAKDOWNS AND RECOVERY

An AA patrolman phones in from the box at Churston, Devon.

One of the greatest challenges since motoring began was to persuade your car to start. I remember many years ago towing a 1909 Rover up and down a country lane for a whole delightful afternoon, with pauses to tinker with the insides of the engine once in a while by way of variety. It never gave any signs of life!

If, like me, you were born and brought up in a large, cold, draughty house, then there would be one room which was kept warm and snug through the winter months, and that was your garage, for that was where your treasure spent its leisure hours.

Your car would be covered with a dustsheet, and with an old blanket or eiderdown over the bonnet. A radiator muff was fitted to the radiator grille, and newspaper or an old blanket surrounded the spark plugs to avoid dreaded condensation. Finally, if you were a bit safety conscious, a tubular electric heater was placed beneath the engine. If you were quite happy-go-lucky, you had a small paraffin heater, and the combination of a naked flame, and a little petrol dripping from a bad connection on the carburettor could have very exciting results!

If you wished to go for a trip in the car, you would first undress it, making soothing noises the while. You would check all fluid levels, and then go and fetch the kettle, gently simmering on the hob, and carefully fill the radiator with lovely hot water. A warm glow would spread through the engine. Then came the cunning bit. You would pretend that you had had second thoughts about going out.

A cold morning, so help from the family required! My first car, a 1935 Morris 8 Tourer, setting off in 1956.

An AA patrolman helps out two young ladies whose Morris Minor has developed a problem.

Perhaps go to your work bench, and busy yourself with a screwdriver. When you had lulled the car into a sense of false security, you would seize the starting handle, insert it, and wind. My present 1946 car, Tess, lets me wind about six times and then gives a twitch. This says 'Swing now, and you might be lucky.' Polly, my wife's 1957 Austin A35 was not nearly so polite, and several times nearly swung me into the dustbin!

But if this does not succeed, then what? You have four options. Go back into the house, admit defeat and find a good book.

Second, try a hill start. Devon, where I lived, is all hills, and we lived on the side of a small one.

The trick was to leave your car overnight in the top stable if you anticipated trouble, so that you could give it a push, jump in, and coast down the yard and out into the road. You needed someone on traffic duty to make sure the road was clear. You then turned right down the hill, setting the controls, putting the car in third or top gear, and letting in the clutch. After 300 yards there is a T junction, and you must turn left to keep the hill. You needed another family member on traffic duty!

If you have not started the car by the time you get to Bramblemoor Cottage, you have only a hundred yards to go before you have a dead car at the bottom of the hill instead of the top. It often did work, but I remember being towed back up the hill

by the local farmer with his tractor on a number of occasions!

Suppose you do not have a hill? In the dread winter of 1962–63 I was living in Cambridge, which is a very flat sort of place! I was able to have a car, and a friend of mine noticed what an advantage a car was for attracting the attention of the lovely nurses of Addenbrookes Hospital, so he promptly went out and bought a pre-war Morris 8. It had to sit out in West Road all winter, and when he decided to go for a drive one morning, the car decided against it, very firmly.

My friend was a small man, but very determined and good at organising others. He promptly rounded up three members of the College Rugby team, all hefty forwards, and bade them come out and push. He climbed into the front seat, the three rugby players tried to get a good grip on the icy snowy road, and they were off. I, being a coward, watched from a second floor window!

After pushing for about twenty yards, the driver let in the clutch, the car juddered to a sudden halt, and the three rugby forwards sprawled in the road. They picked themselves up, and stimulated by commands from the driver, tried again, with exactly the same result. So they continued down the street, until they had nearly run out of road. I then saw the three sportsmen go into a 'huddle.' I could not hear what they said to one another, but the gist must have been 'do it or bust.' For the last time they scrummed down and gave it their all. And suddenly the little car shot away, leaving the players sprawling. But there was no sign of smoke or steam from the exhaust, and the car slowed to a stop. The driver climbed out, looking very vexed, and was joined by his team. I also went down to see what had happened.

The owner of the little car had had very little driving experience, and he had been trying to start the car in bottom gear. This was more effective that using the brakes. The exercise had therefore become a contest of man versus machine, and man had won! The three rugby players had stripped every tooth off the crown wheel in the differential, and the poor little car never again had any connection between its engine and rear wheels!

Nevertheless, it can be done in the right gear, and I have seen, and shared in, many a successful outcome.

The final method requires two drivers, and a live car as well as the dead one. You also need a tow rope, and binder twine won't do, as I witnessed a year or so ago!

Tow ropes come in two types. They are either too long or too short. If the rope is too long, it enables the towing car to achieve a speed of say twenty-five miles an hour before the rope tightens. When it does, either it will snap, or else it will pull a number of pieces off both cars. If, however, the driver of the towing car is skilled, and takes up the slack rope carefully, you can move off in a dignified manner. You may then come to a corner, and find that the towing car has disappeared round it, leaving you in the second car wondering if there is still something on the other end of your rope!

The too short tow rope means that before you move at all you have the impression that you are kissing the car in front. When you move off, the driver of the towing car will open his window so that he can hear what is going on. In the rear car you switch on, set your controls, engage top gear, and when you have reached a good speed, you gently let in the clutch. After a couple of wheezes, the engine bursts into life. At once one foot disengages the clutch, while the other presses the accelerator to keep the engine running. In the front car the driver hears the welcome roar from behind, and knowing his job is done, applies the brakes.

As the driver behind does not usually have a third foot for the brake pedal, the result is a healthy scrunch, which remodels back and front of both cars in quite a spectacular way.

Flooding on the Quay at Bideford in the 1950s. The Austin 10 appears to have succumbed.

However, when properly applied, all of these methods can work very well, and many a sulking car has been goaded into life on a cold morning using one of them.

Breakdowns can be caused by some fault within the car, or a hazard on the road, or a combination of the two. For example, it is a fact that all cars, and especially petrol driven cars, do not like water. Deep water can be terminal.

The problem with most floods is that you can never tell how deep the water is, and once you have decided to try your luck, there is no going back! The rule always is keep going, but gently so that your bow wave does not cause unnecessary damage, or throw water over your distributer, coil and plugs. In the photograph below it appears that another Austin convertible of about 1948 vintage is managing to keep moving, but it is hard to tell.

Bolton Cross, Brixham, in the early 1950s, and a tricky voyage for an Austin 10.

When Motoring Was Fun

Flooding at Fordton, near Crediton, Devon, probably in 1926. A bullnose Morris hesitates to take the plunge.

In many country areas stone bridges cross rivers, and the road rises to cross the bridge. On each side of the road are water meadows, which will easily flood if the river bursts its banks. The bridge can then become a small island surrounded by floods, which will meet across the road and pose a difficult challenge as seen in the photograph above. I don't know whether the vehicles are going to risk it, but the man sitting on the wall looks very settled and not going anywhere.

In a similar situation the local farmer had left his hay bales, all done up in plastic, out in one of the meadows, and the flood water took them all down for a swim and they ended up providing a very effective dam across the bridge.

Water can have a lot of power and it is surprising how well a car will float in some circumstances. In areas where there are frequent flash floods, like the tropics, cars are often swept away when trying to ford rivers that have no bridges. It is a horrible feeling when you realise your wheels are no longer touching the bottom.

In the photograph below a Morris Minor of about 1955 vintage has been swept down by a flooding river and deposited on a bridge in Coldrick, near Sidmouth, close to the river ford. The amount of damage the flood water has done can be clearly seen.

Aftermath of the 1960 floods for a Morris Minor at Coldrick, near Sidmouth.

An Austin Champ with civilian passenger on the Castle-martin Range, Pembrokeshire, above Freshwater West Bay, in 1961.

Clean water may not be so bad, but all too often water is combined with either soil or sand, and that is when the trouble starts.

Freshwater West is a beautiful and large beach in western Wales, gently shelving, and with a tide that goes out at least half a mile. There had been a westerly gale, as was often the case, when I got an urgent call from the Artillery Regiment in Pembroke Dock.

'Have you got a recovery vehicle?'

'Well, I have one of sorts, it's a Matador Gun Tractor.'

'Please get along to Freshwater West urgently. Two of our vehicles are in trouble on the beach.'

I got two helpers and a tow rope, and we climbed into the Matador and trundled off along the coast road at our best speed, which was about 20mph! By the time we arrived it was too late.

The story was that two Austin Champs needed to be road tested after repair, so the drivers decided a trip to Freshwater West would be pleasant, and having arrived, and finding it low tide, suggested a race across the sand. They started well, but after a quarter of a mile one of the Champs came to a grinding halt. Its repair had unravelled. The drivers backed the other one up and attached a tow rope, but because of a seized gearbox they only succeeded in digging the towing vehicle into the sand.

Having no bucket and spade with them, and only a few tools, they then decided to try and free the first vehicle. They were lying underneath it, investigating its gearbox, when the first playful wave lapped round their ears. It always amazes me how quickly the tide comes in on that beach, and by the time they had got to a telephone the vehicles were inches deep in water.

I arrived at about the same time as the Colonel and other officers from the Regiment, and I watched from the shelter of my cab as they watched the waves roll their Champs in a businesslike way up the beach.

Early Days on the Open Road

It was some time after high tide that we were able to get recovery vehicles on to the beach, and we found the Champs looking as though a giant with huge power had held them in his hand and squeezed them, so that nothing which had projected on the Champs was left. I heard that it took a long time to fill in all the forms explaining what had happened.

Incidentally, the Austin Champ was equipped with a snorkel, and when suitably prepared was supposed to be able to be driven underwater, but I never heard of anyone brave enough to try it!

The other hazard on the road that causes frequent trouble is of course snow. I am not sure why we make such a fuss about it, it has been around since long before the motor car. I am able to remember the winter of 1947 in Devon, so the following photograph rings a bell.

Actually, a 1930s Austin Seven would probably be very good in snow. It had large wheels, and an engine with a lot of torque, and a very low bottom gear, as I have mentioned. The next best thing to a tractor, really!

1947 was the winter we all remember above all, when the snow came between Christmas and New Year, and was still around in May. In country areas the often sunken lanes and roads simply filled up as the snow drifted across the fields, as the picture below shows. Motorists fitted chains to their wheels, took some food and drink with them, perhaps something warming to keep their spirits up, and set off into the white world saying they were going out and might be some time.

I remember one car which got caught in a mini blizzard, and remained under a snowdrift for several weeks. I think the owner had forgotten where he left it. Tractors were essential not only for getting about, but for clearing the roads and towing out cars that were stuck. I remember going to a party at a farmhouse, and being met by the owner with his tractor at the bottom of the drive, and ferried up to the house sitting perched on the mudguards. I also remember, a little less clearly, the wonderful hot punch brewed up for us as a welcome on our arrival!

Even in Devon in 1947 we managed to get around somehow, perhaps because our goals were very modest. But comfort when motoring in winter was quite another thing, as very few cars had heaters. We wore caps and huge coats, and leather driving gauntlets to stop our hands freezing to the steering wheel as I have mentioned, but boots served a special purpose. In the early years many cars had the stem of the clutch and brake pedal disappearing through a hole in the floor, and this hole was sealed with a rubber grommet. This appliance was skilfully designed to perish and drop out after about three years, leaving a considerable gap around the pedal stem. This meant that in winter a gentleman could be assured of a jet of icy air up his trouser leg, unless he took steps to prevent it. I am not sure where ladies got it, but my mother always wore a pair of substantial fur lined boots.

Of course if you were driving through melting snow or heavy rain the air was replaced at intervals with a jet of icy water, which was much more unpleasant! All in all we must have been quite a hardy race.

The Clements, of Manaton, Devon, in their Austin 7 do their paper round in the severe winter of 1947.

The winter of 1947, and a tractor clears the road near Sculthorpe, Norfolk, while a Ford V8 Station Wagon waits to get past.

A pre-war Riley resting in the square at Bakewell in the winter of 1947.

The graphic picture above sums up the situation to perfection. Notice how the front of the Riley below the radiator grille has scooped up the snow on its journey. Incidentally, there is something a little odd about the right side headlight, it almost looks as though it is still fitted with the wartime mask. Perhaps the owner simply couldn't get it off because it was rusted in place, or perhaps he didn't know the war had ended!

There were other hazards of the road like fog and wild animals which could cause either difficult or terminated journeys. Rabbits and squirrels one took in one's stride, but a deer could stop you in your tracks, and it's tracks as well, as we found out on one sad occasion.

Our old cars had a number of gauges and similar instruments, and the one that was always regarded with the most suspicion was the fuel gauge. Most people felt theirs was an inveterate liar. Either it would show nothing in the tank, and one could still drive for a hundred miles, or else it would show half a tank full, and then you would run out of petrol! Some drivers resorted to carrying a length of cane or wood so that they could take soundings in the tank , but to do this you had to have a straight petrol filler pipe.

Sometimes the car was to blame. We rescued Alberta, a Riley 1½ litre RME from a basement garage in Hastings, and restored her. Finally came the great day for her maiden run, and with a full fuel tank we set out for a spring day in the country. We found an ideal spot for a picnic lunch, and then meandered on along country lanes until we were heading for home about 4pm and ran out of petrol. Getting some more was a considerable nuisance, with walking and borrowing a can, but we made it home at last. Research over the next few weeks showed that Alberta had what could have been euphemistically described as a bad drink problem, about eleven miles to the gallon.

Sometimes it was not the fault of the car. When I owned my first Hillman Husky, Roddy, I was doing my National Service and was posted to Pembroke Dock. This was very inconvenient, as for personal reasons I wished to make frequent visits to Ipswich, at the far side of the country. The answer was to travel at night. A 48-hour pass might give you from 9pm Friday night to 0630 hours Monday morning for parade, but not a moment longer.

Going east was no problem, but travelling west on a Sunday night was. For some reason no garage in the whole of Wales would serve you so much as a drop of petrol on a Sunday night. We had to fill Roddy to the brim at the bridge at Gloucester (5½ gallons) and then do 132 miles to the barracks at Pembroke Dock. Roddy, with four ample lads on board, would do about 24mpg. As you can see, it's not a very comforting sum!

The answer was to coast down the hills, of which Wales has very many. In those days if you switched off your engine and coasted you did not lose the use of your power steering, or the use of your power assisted brakes. But I did find that I lost about half of the power of my not very good headlights! So there I would be, speeding down a hill at anything up to forty miles per hour, peering into the darkness. And it was then that I made an interesting discovery. The average Welsh sheep delights to sleep in the middle of the road. As I peered forward, I would suddenly spy a large white woolly bundle, and have to take an instant decision as to which side of it to go. I must say the sheep were amazing. Even if I passed a couple of inches away, they never stirred, and I don't think I ever caught a strand of wool on my wing mirror.

We always made it safely to Pembroke Dock in time for first parade, but I think sometimes we had about a mug full of petrol left in the tank!

The old-fashioned petrol engine depended on two things: roughly the right mixture of fuel and air entering the cylinder, and a spark being applied at about the right moment. I have mentioned the electrical side, where a very small defect or adjust-

Polly, my wife's Austin A35, of 1957 vintage, kept us on our toes with several unusual habits!

ment could make a huge difference to the performance of your engine. One always carried precision tools like an old nail file for attending to the points or plugs.

The fuel was a very different creature. Petrol tanks rusted over a long period, being slung usually in a very exposed position behind the back wheels, and the fuel which one bought could also have come out of an ancient tank. As a result, the fuel pumped along to the carburettor could contain a lot of muck, only some of which was filtered out along the way.

Then there was the fuel pump itself, always a very temperamental animal. Some, mounted in the engine, tried to suck the fuel up. Others, mounted beside the fuel tank, pushed it through to the engine. They could be mechanical or electric, diaphragm or other. Diaphragms had a limited life and would split without warning. Some cars seemed to build up a vacuum somewhere along the fuel line, or in the tank.

Polly, our Austin A35, did a regular morning run accompanying my wife to Shoreham Hospital. She started fine, but about two miles down the road began to lose power, and my wife always turned into the same convenient lay-by, and there Polly died. My wife would let her rest for a couple of minutes, then start her up, and have no further problems for the rest of the day!

What made this habit even more strange was that when we moved to Suffolk it ceased, and never occurred again as long as we had the lively little car!

Another cause of problems would be the blocking of the carburettor jets. Muck that got through the fuel filter would wholly or partially block a jet, either causing the engine to die, or the car to progress in a series of kangaroo leaps. The solution was simple. You unscrewed the jets and 'blew them out!' In a garage the mechanics would use the airline, but you had to hold on to the jet tightly, or you would be on your hands and knees looking for something much smaller than a thimble among all the debris on the garage floor!

There was one other part of the engine that required the skills of a plumber and odd job man combined, and that was the cooling system. The earlier cars, like my Tess, did not have a water pump or pressurised system, but just relied on the circulating properties of water being heated up and cooled down. They were much the better for this simplicity.

As soon as more sophisticated systems were introduced, the problems multiplied. Radiator caps could leak, and let water out of the overflow pipe. Hoses would be more likely to leak. The water pump, with its mixture of moving parts and water under pressure was always a source of trouble. The thermostat was a law to itself, often open when it should have been closed, and vice-versa. Finally, the water pump was driven off the fanbelt, placing additional strain on this piece of rubber, and causing it to bust at the most inconvenient moment. A baleful red light would appear on your dashboard, and you would know the worst.

Another cause of problems, when your lorry is too big for the road. Porlock Hill, Somerset.

Prudent motorists would carry a spare fanbelt about with them, and I do remember doing so for a time with one car. But then there was the story that if your fanbelt broke, you could substitute a pair of your wife's tights, or a silk stocking. I confess that I never believed this story, as I had some idea of the tension required to make a fanbelt function, and I never remember seeing ladies descending from vehicles with one stocking off and one stocking on!

However, I mentioned this at a gathering on one occasion, and was quickly put right. The car was a Ford Anglia, the tights were of the best quality, and they did duty for the fanbelt for several weeks until the owner of the car could save up the necessary 9/6d to buy a new belt. After use on the car, however, the tights were not deemed suitable for their original purpose any more!

The other interesting feature of the cooling system was its ability to boil, and produce spectacular quantities of steam. If you let it do too much of this it would boil dry, and your engine would overheat and seize up completely, which was most undesirable.

The cooling system relied to a considerable extent on a nice current of air passing through the radiator. Very slow progress up a steep hill, or sitting in a traffic jam with the engine running, could both cause the engine to boil. You had to stop the engine, allow it to cool down a bit, then add more cold water, but very gently. On one occasion with Roddy I took off the radiator cap too quickly, and sprayed my face with near boiling water. Luckily a nearby hospital rectified the situation as far as my face was concerned, but I never made that mistake again.

Overheating also showed up weaknesses in one's hoses, and here wire, hose clips, and tape were often pressed into service to get one home.

Not long ago, while driving Tess in overlarge sandals, I got my foot jammed under the break pedal while double declutching on a steep hill, and over revved the engine, to the point where the fan spun off the front and carved a chunk out of the radiator before falling into the road. Tess became at once totally incontinent. We retrieved the fan, and limped to a nearby house, where we begged a can of water. By quickly filling up the radiator, and setting off at once, we covered about a mile. Fortunately another house, and another gave us water, and we just made it home. The radiator had to be removed and rebuilt, and it did need attention anyway.

Our radiators did gradually get bunged up with rust and other muck, and there were exciting mixtures you could pour into them, with names like Raddiphart, or Raddipurge, which were supposed to give them a total catharsis. Taking the radiator out, turning it upside down, and running the garden hose at full pressure through it for some time seemed to do better than anything else I tried. It did make rather a mess on the lawn, however.

Engines could produce lots of other tricks of course. A look at the exhaust pipe could tell a tale. Clouds of blue smoke indicated very worn pistons, and the need for a re-bore or the fitting of piston rings. Clouds of steam would indicate that the cylinder head gasket was leaking badly, - another plumbing job, but harder. Gauges in the car showing oil pressure and water temperature would also alert you to the fact that all was not well under your bonnet.

Finally, if there was no way you could fix the problem by the roadside, even by using your wife's corset or suspender belt, then you had to organise some sort of recovery to get your beloved motor car back to the haven of a garage.

In the early days you called up a horse or two, and they did the job with a nasty smirk on their faces! As motor transport developed, a lorry or tractor became the preferred method, and in due course specialist breakdown lorries with small cranes on the back were developed. But in spite of this, many a recovery was done with the assistance of a friend or family member, and a tow rope, with all the tow rope excitements already mentioned! I remember the satisfaction of recovering my Ford Cortina, suffering from a defunct clutch, using my 1946 Sunbeam Talbot to tow it home!

I can even remember tales of people who had not got a tow rope of any kind, but who got their dead car pushed by a friend to a local garage. In those days our bumpers, fore and aft, were significantly

Early Days on the Open Road

RAC Patrolmen on duty in Devon, in the 1960s, prepared for a busy day of holiday traffic.

stronger than today's and if you didn't mind a scratch or two on the chrome you could do it quite well.

In those days we did not have the 'get you home' insurance of today, so one got towed in to the nearest garage, and they would fix the problem for you. I remember managing to limp into Bexley off the A2 with a clutch on its last legs, and the car was ready to roll, fully repaired in about 3 hours.

In another chapter I shall dwell on the rather more spectacular ways of terminating a journey!

There was always one other way of failing to achieve your journey's end, and that was by the simple expedient of getting lost en route!

The ability to cultivate a sense of direction, and to read a map, was always a great help to the motorist. You could carry a compass, but though this is ideal on a ship, the winding nature of roads did not always help. Steering by the sun or stars required cloudless conditions which could not be guaranteed.

It helped if your map was reasonably up to date. In about 1994 some friends visited, and we went for a drive of exploration, with myself as the navigator, armed with Ordnance Survey map. All through the countryside I was able to point out features marked on the map, as well as country roads. But when we were approaching our home town, I had a problem.

'Ron' I said, 'The sign there says there's a road coming which is not marked on my map at all.'

'What date is your map?' asked Ron, our driver.

I looked at the bottom of the map.

'It looks like 1917' I admitted! It was one of my father's old maps which I had inherited. Up to that moment the map had been perfectly accurate, which must say something about the unchanging nature of the Suffolk countryside, thank goodness!

Getting lost could be very easy indeed in certain circumstances. One New Year, about 1954, my mother took a party of us to London to see some shows. We travelled again in the faithful Land Rover, which lacked a heater, so lots of rugs were essential.

We went to see a wonderful pantomime on ice at the Haringey Arena, and as it was a matinée performance we came out about 4.30pm and found London enveloped in a superb quality 'pea-souper' fog. We had to try and get back to Tottenham, so we started off, and for some reason mother decided to follow the red lights of the car in front.

This vehicle we had chosen to be our pathfinder behaved in a rather curious manner. It would travel half a mile or so, and then stop for a couple of minutes. At length we closed up a bit, and by the light of a street lamp were able to see we had been following a postman who was busy collecting the afternoon post from the letter boxes! At that point the fog lifted a bit, and we eventually found our way back to base.

Motorists can become very attached to their vehicles, and the prospect of abandoning your poor car either in a flood or snowdrift, or because it had broken down, was often akin to abandoning a beloved relative or friend.

When Motoring Was Fun

The author's father consults his road map in about 1935, while his Hillman 14 Tourer waits for his decision.

Motorists would wait in their cars for rescue, often getting very cold and hungry in the process. However, it was the case that more people carried hip flasks with something warming in them in those days.

Our cars could also catch fire, and did. An old cousin of mine had a much worn and neglected old Ford van which he used for fishing trips to Ireland. He christened it 'The Rabbit'. On one occasion when returning from his fishing trip smoke began to issue from under the dashboard. My cousin stopped at once, leaped out of the van and began to run up the road. In a nearby field a group of people were getting in the crop, and my cousin shouted to them 'Help! Help! The rabbit's on fire.'

Needless to say they hadn't a clue what he was talking about, and it took some time before he was able to explain to them what the problem really was. They then all streamed down the road, but found to their disappointment that the conflagration had ceased once the ignition had been turned off!

I was also told the story of the music mistress setting off on a journey in her Morris Minor Traveller. The cars rear doors were open, the back seat flat, and an old mattress on the floor. Her pupils watched as she carried her precious cello out of the music school, placed it in the back of the car, and covered it with an old shawl. She then went and fetched mother, aged 93, and piloted her into the front passenger seat. Having closed all doors, she then started the engine, and began to warm it up,

and it was amazing how quickly the old blanket she had wrapped round the spark plugs, and forgotten to remove, caught fire! Smoke eddied out from beneath the bonnet of the Morris.

Being an intelligent driver she at once switched off the engine. Then she leapt out, rushed to the back, opened the doors and lifting out her cello, took it inside to a place of comfort and safety. She then returned and extracted her mother, who was much nearer the scene of the trouble, and took her back inside as well!

Finally, there was often a problem of brakes, already alluded to with my Austin 7. My mother taped some reminiscences, and this one from about 1920, sheds more light on the problems.

We had two punctures on the journey, so called in at Bodmin, and while they fixed the car Robin gave me lunch at the Royal Hotel. It was my idea to buy four new tyres. When we eventually got to St Tudy they had kept our lunch warm for us. We were not popular! And then, as we drove back, going down Charles Hill the brakes wouldn't hold, so I was turned out of the car by the road, and Robin came down the hill, not sitting in the car but running beside it, holding on to the steering wheel with one hand, and pulling on the handbrake with the other. How he arrived intact at the bottom I'll never know, but he did!

To a young maiden of mother's age it must have seemed great fun.

Chapter 8

THE CAR MAKERS

The Clement Talbot Car chassis workshop, Barlby Road, Notting Hill in 1905.

As we have already noted, the early car manufacturers in this country and abroad had a wide variety of beginnings, but all had the vision to see that the motor car was here to stay, and to see the possibilities for cars if they could be made safe, reliable and relatively cheap.

At first it was a struggle. As Laurence Pomeroy, a noted motoring enthusiast and expert wrote: 'From 1885 to 1895 men struggled to make the car go. From 1896 to 1905 they contrived to make it go properly.' After 1905 the car makers realised two important facts about their cars. First, that an almost infinite number of combinations of features could be built into a motor car, so that no two vehicles need ever be the same. Second, that their products, their cars, would go out on the roads of the world to advertise for them their engineering genius, their sense of style, and their value for money.

From a very early stage the car makers began to take a great pride in their creations, and to make their cars as distinctive as possible so that they would be instantly recognised. Rolls-Royce early adopted the triangular radiator top. Daimler had a fluted radiator top. Vauxhall had very distinctive chrome flutes on each side of the bonnet which made them easy to recognise. Renault favoured a sloping front to the bonnet which was different to any other car. Lastly cars like the 'Bullnose' Morris Cowley, the Austin 7, and the Model T Ford were just so distinctive, as well as widespread, that everyone who was remotely interested in motor cars knew them on sight.

As the car makers strove for recognition, they also realised that a car owner's loyalty to a particular make of car was a very important advantage. Men especially came to see owning and driving a car as an important indicator to status, and therefore their ability to judge the worth of a particular make of car mattered a lot. Conversations in the pub of an evening might go as follows:

Fred (clutching pint) ' Got a real surprise today, old man.'

When Motoring Was Fun

Final assembly of Clement Talbot cars, Barlby Road factory, Notting Hill, in about 1905.

'Arthur (also clutching pint) 'What was that old man?'

Fred (making theatrical pause, and taking a large swig) 'I took delivery of my new car this morning. Another Rover (Ford/Vauxhall/Austin) of course. Took her out on the Ridgeway, put my foot down and she was up to seventy in no time. And not even run in yet!'

Each car maker would have their own network of dealers, who had a franchise to sell that particular make of car, and the two would work closely together to promote the maker's products. The dealer would get 'inside information' about a new car coming on to the market shortly, and could thus chat up a customer.

Dealer: 'There you are, Mr Sprocket, your car is all checked and serviced as you requested.'

Mr Sprocket (who likes to think he knows all about cars, but can't tell a crankshaft from a back axle): 'Everything all right, I hope.'

Dealer (pauses, as though fighting an inner battle): 'I wouldn't be honest with you, Mr Sprocket, if I didn't mention that I am a bit worried about the pistons. Especially numbers two and four cylinders.' (It could just as well be one and three, no one is ever going to know!)

Mr Sprocket (alarmed): 'What is the trouble?'

Dealer: 'She's using a lot of oil sir, as you can see by the exhaust. Start her up, Bob.'

Bob, who has just spilt a little engine oil into the float chamber of the carburettor, obliges. All three men disappear in a cloud of blue smoke.

Mr Sprocket: 'My goodness, thank heavens you spotted that. I had not noticed it myself.'

Dealer (sorrowfully): 'Very few drivers know what is coming out of their exhausts, sir.'

Mr Sprocket (pretty terrified): 'Will she get me home? What do you advise?'

Dealer (after careful consideration): 'I think she'll manage that, sir, but in the long term, there's going to be a lot of work needed on this car. Expensive work, too, sir.'

Mr Sprocket: 'Oh dear, oh dear!'

Dealer (moving in for the kill): 'There is one thing I feel I ought to share with you, sir. I heard only yesterday that Viking are bringing out a new model next week. It's very hush hush, few people know. Now, if you thought of trading in this old car (he restrains himself from giving it a kick) I think I could obtain one of the new models for you, even though it would be the first in this district.'

The thought of being able to boast that he has the first of the new Viking models in the district is the clincher for Mr Sprocket, and the dealer, who knows his man, is well aware of the fact. So the deal is done, and Mr Sprocket's old car, all spruced up and with the carburettor cleaned out does not take long to leave the showroom. Mr Sprocket impresses all who see him with his gleaming new car, except his bank manager.

Early Days on the Open Road

The scene in the machine shop of the Clement Talbot Works in Barby Road, Notting Hill, about 1905.

When people travelled much more locally, and garages were fewer, drivers would stick to a dealer and the make of car he sold.

The principle of factory production was well established by the time the car came on the scene, as the photographs of the Clement Talbot works show. Henry Ford had shown the way very early on, and other car makers tried to introduce assembly line principles to their manufacturing procedure.

However, cars still had to be hand built to a large extent, as their construction involved a mixture of metal, wood and fabric, with heavy elements like engines and gearboxes. The early photograph of the Model T Ford assembly line, which shows the bodies being delivered on one conveyor belt and then dropped on to the waiting chassis below does not conceal the fact that a good deal of adjustment had to be done by the fitters who put the two together. It must have been quite a lottery as to how well each fitted, and I can imagine many a sigh of relief when it was almost perfect, and some fairly ripe language when a lot of adjustment and packing was required.

The men who did this work were all engineers, and many had great talent and years of experience. In many of the smaller factories parts had to be machined to a very precise specification, and there was no room for shoddy work. The photograph above shows how many men would have been involved in this work, and also the types of machines they used. The belts used to drive drills and lathes from overhead power shafts were typical of many different kinds of factories of this period. Health and Safety was not given quite the priority it is today, but the men used a lot of common sense.

The development of the car industry could be described as a series of fits and starts. At one moment production is greatly limited by the time it took to make a car, and there were a fair number of customers. Then in a year or two came a war, and all production of cars was diverted for military use. Then the car makers got going again only to find that stock market crash and depression had made customers wary of spending a small fortune on a motor car.

For the smaller companies this lack of consistency in the market, and resulting variations in cash flow, made life very difficult, and it is not surprising that a number became casualties. Some of these companies simply disappeared. Others were snapped up by their bigger rivals, who felt the name was worth having, or who spotted one or two useful patents for features which could be incorporated into their own cars.

From the start Ford set the example of a multinational car manufacturing company, and the Model T Ford is an excellent example of what a company could do in this respect. The car was in production from 1910 to 1927, and by the end over 15 million examples of the model had been sold all over the world. In the end the cost of a chassis was down to £105, and a 4/5 seater tourer cost only £125.

Talbot's private test track running round the outside of the factory complex, with new cars on test. Barlby Road, Notting Hill, c.1910.

In addition to this, Henry Ford recognised the great importance of a fully comprehensive spares service, and spares could be posted to any part of the world, so that owners or the local blacksmith could easily repair a Model T Ford and get it back on the road again.

I have already written about the aristocrats of the motoring world, and also about the baby cars, which had a habit of growing larger as the years went by. In the middle were a large group of car makers, producing a wide variety of models. We can also see a distinct variation in design and practice in different parts of the world. France and Germany had been the cradle of the motoring industry, in part thanks to ridiculously restrictive laws in force in Britain. The United States, thanks in part to Henry Ford, were quick to catch up, and here William Durant set a far seeing precedent. He was determined to build up a huge car making corporation, and between 1917 and 1921 he founded General Motors Corporation, which incorporated Buick, Cadillac, Oakland, Oldsmobile and Chevrolet.

In 1921 Durant took over the Opel Company in Germany, and in 1925 he took over Vauxhall motors in England. This was a very significant operation as a guide to the future of the motor industry, as it showed a number of companies being acquired and arranged within one group, and also the acquisition of foreign companies which would henceforth be the bridgehead for penetrating the markets of other countries.

Different countries also developed characteristics of their own with regard to design and practice. The USA being a country with cheap fuel and large distances tended to produce large cars with the emphasis on space and comfort. Much later, when I was working as a tourist guide using my Hillman Imp, I picked up two American visitors from Glasgow station. When we got outside the station and approached my waiting car, Mr Yontz stopped and stared at it.

'I guess, Tom,' he drawled, 'this would just about fit in the trunk of my car back home!'

The US carmakers also pioneered the idea of the disposable car. 'Build a car that will last for ever, like Rolls-Royce' they said, 'and where is the profit in that? You want your car to fall to bits in five years, by which time you have a super new model to replace it!'

On the Continent there were a wide range of models produced, some with quite radical ideas. In France the Citroen 'Traction Avant' front-wheel drive saloons were a great success, and a pointer to the future. This company was later to produce the striking DS19 saloon, with its rising suspension system, which always looked a bit strange but worked very well. In Germany the designer Porsche conceived the Volkswagen, the 'peoples car' in the 1930s. With its streamlined 'beetle' shape, and flat four rear engine, which was air cooled, it was a brilliant design that was to last for many many years.

In Britain, as on the continent, car makers struggled to read the public mind and produce the car that would appeal at the price people could afford. Sadly, some makers could not compete, and either disappeared or were swallowed up. William Rootes who founded the Rootes Group, started with Hillman Cars, and then acquired Humber, Singer, Sunbeam and Talbot, and finally in the commercial department Commer and Karrier. Meanwhile Austin and Morris eventually amalgamated under the name of a commercial vehicle maker, and became British Leyland, and then incorporated other makers like Rover, Riley and Wolseley. The acquisition of Rover was later, for an interesting reason.

The car makers had had a gruelling time during the Second World War, and were now desperate to

The Talbot engine assembly shop, Barlby Road, Notting Hill, c.1930. There are no shaft or belt drives to be seen here.

The generating plant which supplied all the power for the Talbot Factory ar Barlby Road, Notting Hill. Note the very grand plaque on the wall.

replace pre-war models that very much looked their age. Rover opted for the Rover 75, a great big tank of a car with a distinctive single fog light in the centre of the radiator. It was comfortable, stodgy, sturdy, heavy and very thirsty! The public did not take to it, as it was also pretty expensive, without really competing with cars like Alvis, Lagonda and the like.

Rover were on their last legs, saddled with something akin to a large white elephant, when somebody had a bright idea. During the war the Willys Jeep had been a great success, and when the US Army retired back over the water many of these sturdy little vehicles were sold off cheap and left behind. Farmers and others who needed a cross-country performance snapped them up. But the Jeep was not ideal, it too was pretty thirsty, and it actually had very little room in it. Rover came up with a new design, the Land Rover. This was a sort of Jeep, but more comfortable, more economical, and with a good deal more room, especially for cargo, inside. Three people could sit in reasonable comfort across the front, and more could sit behind if a load was not being carried. As we proved with our family trips to Austria, it was amazing what you could pack in. The engine was a standard Rover 4 cylinder, but you could go into low ratio, which halved your speeds in every gear and doubled the power, and you could be in high ratio and engage

4-wheel drive. This gave a lot of options for cross country work, or in mud or snow.

The Land Rover saved Rover. A senior executive at the rival Nuffield organisation, observing what was going on at Rover, remarked: 'Always a bad sign, that sort of thing.' But Austin were forced shortly to follow Rover's lead, bringing out the much heralded Austin Gipsy, which like most copies was a singular flop! The Land Rover went from strength to strength, and still does, so Rover had the last laugh! They proceeded to bring out four more variations on the Rover 75, which were much more successful, culminating in the Rover 2 and 3 litre models which were attractive quality cars.

Meanwhile, at every level of the market in the 1950s, the price of your car continued to be a most important factor. Some manufacturers strove to keep their prices as low as possible, and were prepared to get a reputation for a 'cheap and cheerful' car.

As the car makers consolidated and grouped together, so they used the different traditional names to denote the quality and features of their cars. Thus within the Rootes Group, the Hillman Cars, the Minx, and later the Husky and Imp, were the family cars at the cheap end of the market. Then

The finished Talbot product, a 10/23 model of 1923, being shown off by the film star Gladys Cooper.

might come the Singer Vogue, a larger family car and more luxurious. Sunbeam Talbots, or Sunbeams, represented the sporty side of the repertoire, with rally winners like the Sunbeam Alpine. The Humber range were the most luxurious and largest of the groups products, with cars suitable for royalty, perhaps.

I remember when I lived in the British Solomon Islands, as they then were, and we celebrated the Queens official birthday. Police, troops and dignitaries were all lined up, the royal standard was hoisted and as the Humber limousine glided onto the square the National Anthem was played. An official stepped forward and opened the car door, and the Queen descended to be with her loyal people, only she was invisible to us. After the High Commissioner had inspected the guard, presumably with the Queen at his side, she was escorted back to her car, the door was shut, and the Humber purred away to convey Her Majesty to other of her far flung dominions!

As the years passed, and mass production techniques became ever more sophisticated, the car makers resorted to standardisation of cars as far as possible to keep costs down. For example the British

Motor Corporation would build an 1100 model, the Austin and Morris cars being only really distinguishable by the badge on the front and the name on the back. Then the Riley had a second carburettor, perhaps, a different radiator and colour scheme, and an imitation wood dashboard, while the Wolseley model had the same sort of treatment but retained the illuminated badge at the top of the radiator. This was a very clever idea, as it meant the Wolseley was instantly recognisable at night. The Police, who used them a lot, were not so keen on the idea and often used to remove the bulb behind the translucent badge!

Finally came the top of the range Princess, with real wood dashboard and trim, and real leather seats. The same body shell was used for all the cars, and basically the same engine and transmission as well, which saved a lot of money in the production.

From the start the car makers vied with each other to advertise their models. And at the beginning there was a lot of opposition from the general public to be overcome. In some notorious districts round the country motorists literally ran the gauntlet. S.F. Edge, the famous racing driver, recalled driving past Crawley in Sussex during the winter of 1900, and as he passed by being hit on the head by a rock. Spotting the 'yokel' who had heaved the rock by the light of his acetylene headlamps, Edge stopped his car and gave chase through the snow. Two fields later he caught up with the culprit, being very fit, and he then relieved him of all his clothes except his pants and shoes (he was also a merciful man). These he deposited at the next village up the road. It was, he added with satisfaction, one of the coldest nights of the year!

There is one remarkable and colourful French advertisement for De Dion-Bouton cars, dating from 1899. The picture shows a De Dion-Bouton car being driven along what is, for the period, a busy road. In the background are three quite curious vehicles, and then nearer a De Dion Camionniette (I think) which has been narrowly missed by the speeding car, and its driver nearly unseated. On the left a horse rears up, almost upsetting its cart, and two pigs just escape from beneath the wheels of the speeding car. In the car the front passenger, with her back to us, and her parasol almost totally obscuring the driver's vision, reaches out a hand to the baby. Beside the driver, his attractive wife, with headgear ribbons flying in the wind, is breast feeding her baby, and showing a vast amount of exposed breast in the process. The driver, her husband, (presumably) has eyes for nothing but the baby, or the milk supplier, and certainly none for the road!

This whacky advertisement, in full colour, is almost in line with the incredibly stupid advertisements we are subjected to today on TV by makers trying to sell their cars, but apparently it is very typical of French car adverts at the turn of the twentieth century, the idea was that the car owner and his passengers were set apart from normal life and the mayhem they might be causing on the roads. One can't help a twinge of sympathy for the yokel who hove a rock at Mr Edge!

The advertisement for Rover Cars has a number of interesting features. First, it is an attractive picture, with plenty of detail, and there has been no attempt to depict the car as bigger or faster than it really is. The caption, 'Rover, one of Britain's fine cars' acknowledges that there are other fine cars built in the country. Solihull in Birmingham, and Devonshire House London are mentioned as linked to these cars.

What the advertisement does not tell you is that you can't have a Rover saloon for love or money! In 1939 my father put his name down for one, and in 1952 he was still waiting for it to be delivered. What was really hard to bear was the visit of cousin Hugh Naylor, from Southern Rhodesia, in 1947. He had come over to England to collect his new car,

A very attractive advertisement for a Rover saloon in the period just after the war, c 1946.

and then drove down to Devon to visit us, and 'try the new car out.' I can see my father now, walking round the beautiful green Bentley Sports Saloon in the yard. He didn't dare let himself touch it, and he was about as green as the car!

So we soldiered on with the faithful old Hillman Minx, and it certainly was the car 'for the family whose car is always in use...'

The following advertisement certainly does make the car look bigger than it really was, and from my memory getting all that luggage into the boot might have been quite a conjuring trick, though the post-war Minx did have a bigger boot than the model we had.

The copy of *Motor* magazine for 30 October 1946 is the Motor Show edition and has advertisements for many makes of cars in it. One is very struck by the language used. Singer state 'Our plan takes shape..' and go on to detail production plans for the next year, while admitting that their cars will be in short supply.

Lea-Francis claim 'Style and speed go hand in hand'. Renault talk about comfort and reliability. AC Cars show pictures of models from 1909, via 1925 and 1939 to the latest 1947 model. Armstrong Siddeley are graciously designed, stylish and practical, while Rolls-Royce modestly claim 'The best car in the world.'

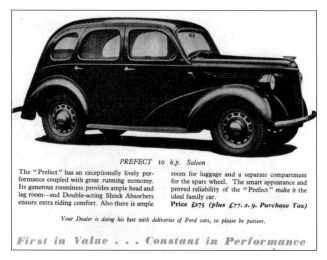

Advertisement for a Ford Prefect in October 1946.

For the family whose car is always in use . . .

The Hillman Minx is a car for the whole family to share . . . safe, easily handled in crowded streets . . . fast, roomy and comfortable on a long drive to the coast . . . quietly dignified for an evening in Town. A car that never runs up costs, that always keeps appointments . . . for the family whose car is always in use.

HILLMAN MINX

1946 advertisement for the Hillman Minx, but could you actually get one?

ing up what was left of the industry, and then showing us how it should have been done, - sometimes.

It is interesting that the once great Austin and Morris Companies merged to become the British Motor Corporation, then became the British Leyland Motor Corporation, then reduced that to British Leyland, which seemed much simpler, and finally, in a last ditch attempt to keep above the surface, resorted to the name Rover. But it was all to no avail.

Riley, by now a member of the Nuffield Group. But still producing a very distinctive range of cars state 'Riley performance, safety and inherent quality blend to give Magnificent Motoring.' Incidentally it is interesting to note the price, £675, to which had to be added £188.5s in purchase tax. That makes our 17.5% V.A.T. seem almost reasonable!

The Ford advertisement is a good example of an advert of the day, with clear and realistic pictures of two of their cars, and then a very accurate write up stressing comfort, performance and the all important economy, petrol was very much rationed still. They also emphasised the price, as excellent value for money. It is a very good factual presentation to impress future owners.

Making cars did not get any easier as the years passed, with global competition, especially from Japan, and with labour problems in the factories at home. In fact the story of the British car makers is one of sad and steady decline, with inspired ideas not being followed up with the necessary investment, and foreign companies stepping in and buy-

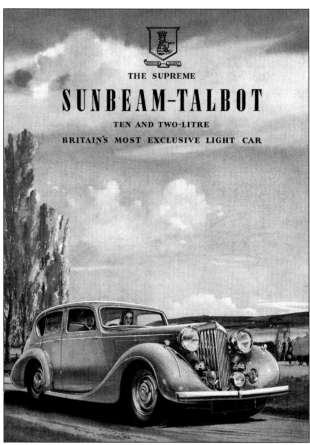

THE SUPREME

SUNBEAM-TALBOT

TEN AND TWO-LITRE

BRITAIN'S MOST EXCLUSIVE LIGHT CAR

An example of a 1946 advertisement for the Sunbeam-Talbot two litre saloon.

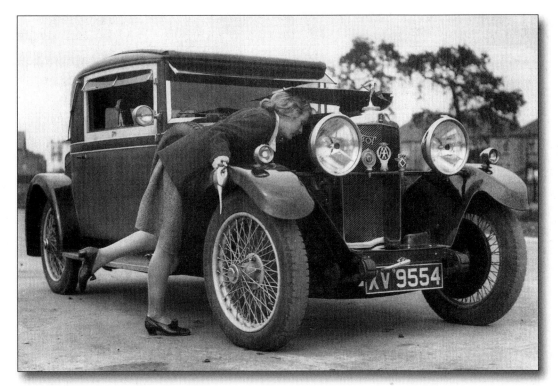

A superb publicity shot from 1929 of 'well known rally driver Kitty Brunel'. Kitty obviously knew what went on under the bonnet of her Talbot 14/45.

One final detail about the car makers is worth noting, and that is that they trusted their car owners. My 1946 Sunbeam Talbot came with a handbook of instructions, which runs to 84 pages. It is a small, convenient book, about 4x7 inches in size, and it is clear and comprehensive. It begins with addresses and telephone numbers at the works, and you could be sure the phone would be answered by a human being in Coventry! After General Data is a table showing the engine revolutions per minute at 14 different speeds in the four forward gears, information essential to a good driver trying to get the best fuel consumption. The book is illustrated with excellent photographs and diagrams, and so well produced that apart from a few stains, engine oil or grease, I suspect, it has survived over 60 years with no problems!

As we have seen, during both wars women as well as men had to come to grips with motor vehicles, and basic servicing was often only the start. My mother used to take the head off the engine of her Model T Ford at regular intervals, de-carbonise the cylinders, and then re-grind the valves into their sockets. This was an essential routine if the performance of the car was to be maintained.

In the 40s and 50s such was my interest in cars that I could recognise every car on sight, and usually from just a view of the radiator. I have to admit that as the graceful pre-war lines gave way to all steel bodies modelled on the American pattern, with gaping radiators and large chrome bumpers, I was disappointed.

Perhaps that is why the Jaguar XK120 was hailed with such enthusiasm when it appeared. Not only was it a marvellously fast car, which outstripped all its rivals, but it had the lines and looks of a truly British car. It was a natural successor to the lovely sports cars of the 1930s.

Mention should be made in this chapter of Morgan cars. Morgan started at Malvern Link in 1909, with a three-wheel car which was distinctive as the engine hung out of the front. In 1936 they produced their first four wheel car, the 4/4. Since then the Morgan cars have had small concessions made to progress, especially in the engine department, but the graceful lines of the car remain essentially as they were in 1936, and people queue up for years to get their hands on one.

The conclusion seems to be that if you design a car that is graceful and has good performance, is comfortable and reliable, there is no need to keep changing your design!

Chapter 9

BITS THAT DROP OFF AND OTHER ACCIDENTS

The 1906 Markyate accident scene, Hertfordshire, with horse and cart in the foreground, and the Peugeot car behind.

The Romans built their great Watling Street as straight as an arrow from London to Chester, and some 25 miles from London the small village of Markyate grew up round the always busy road. In 1723 a Turnpike Trust was set up, and the previously awful road became properly maintained. A coaching inn in the village did good trade until the railways took a lot of the business. In 1906 life went on much as it always had, and a carter had no hesitation in leading his horse and cart out of River Mill Road on to the main road, right into the path of a speeding Peugeot car being driven by a chauffeur from Coventry to London.

It was a major collision, with the horse and a passenger in the cart fatally injured, the cart overturned, and the carter having both legs broken. The car driver emerged unscathed.

In the subsequent court case no blame was attached to the carter who had emerged on to the main road without checking to see if a vehicle was coming. It was the car driver who was in the dock, and much debate centred round the speed he was

doing, and consequently what control he had over the car.

It was established that he had done the journey so far at an average speed of over 25mph which was very fast. Witnesses varied hugely in their estimate of his speed before the accident, from 8mph to 'great speed.' If the road was good, judging from the position of the car and the effect of the impact one would guess 30mph at least.

The chauffeur was convicted of manslaughter, (horse slaughter didn't count!) but because of his previous good record, and the fact that the road sign for the crossroads was hidden behind a telegraph pole and needed repainting, he got off with a lenient sentence of two months imprisonment. One suspects he probably lost his job as well, and would have had great difficulty finding another one.

This accident was perhaps a classic illustration of the collision between the new and the old that was taking place at this moment. From now on the old habits of wandering about in the road, whether in

70

Early Days on the Open Road

The Peugeot car involved in the 1906 Markyate accident, showing the extent of the damage.

possession of a horse and cart or not, would have to change.

One feature of this accident is rather remarkable, and is illustrated by the photograph of the Peugeot car immediately after the accident. It has lost a headlight, and damaged its wings, but the radiator, wheels and springs seem intact. There is also damage to the passenger side front seat, but the steering wheel seems fine, and one feels it could have been driven in that condition. The driver brought the car to a halt 56 yards from the collision, and was unhurt. At the time it was thought the steering wheel had protected him, but looking at the steering wheel it really doesn't offer any protection, and in that exposed position it was amazing he wasn't thrown out and badly hurt. All in all, it is a testimonial to the strength of the new cars, and their well engineered construction.

Sadly, Markyate had been in the news only the previous year, as the first 'hit and run' accident occurred there. Willie Clifton, aged four, was hit and killed by a car outside his home in London Road. The car did not stop, and the incident caused a local and national furore. Sir Alfred Harmsworth, the owner of the *Daily Mail*, offered a reward of £100 for information on the driver of the car involved. After enquiries by Hertfordshire Police and Scotland Yard, it was discovered that the driver of the car was Rocco Cornalbas, a Spanish chauffeur employed by Mr Hildebrand Harmsworth, brother of Sir Alfred!

General embarrassment all round, and the reward was not paid! Rocco was tried at the Hertfordshire Assizes in July 1905, and sentenced to six months' hard labour, which seems excessively lenient. One wonders whether the Harmsworths had again intervened?

Poor little Willie Clifton was given as grand a funeral as the village could manage, and one suspects that the people of Markyate had a very poor opinion of chauffeurs for many years to come.

Accidents in rural areas were always going to be remembered. Not far from the Devon village where I grew up there was a four crossroads where two lanes met, and neither had a right of way. In the mid 1930s my father, driving his Hillman 14, came to the crossroads, and moved slowly across just at the precise moment that a motorcyclist came down the intersecting road. The timing could not have been more precise, and my father saw the rider do a graceful dive over the bonnet of the car. He was fortunate to live to tell the tale, but thereafter the spot was known as 'Crash Corner' in our family, and never forgotten.

My mother also had a tale to tell among her Cornish memories:

Some time after the first world war my father was asked to take a wedding in Penzance, and I drove him as far as Truro, and put him on a train. In the evening I met him and we set off for home. The main road to Truro was closed for some reason, and we had to take the Mitchell road, a road I had never been on. It was a dark and misty night, and the car lights were very poor, but I thought I could see where the road widened out ahead, and assumed it was the junction with the other Truro road, which would have been alright, you see. I then saw this car standing at the side of the road, with a road light on, so I gave it six to eight inches clearance, and the next thing we had tipped right over into a duck pond, and my father, who was sitting next to me, was thrown right over me and into the middle of the pond. The duck pond was about eighteen inches deep, but my father was unhurt, despite the hood being smashed to bits.

They came running out from the nearby farm asking 'is it alright. Is anyone underneath?'

I said 'No, but I've lost my shoe!' They finally found it after about half an hour, and brought it into the farmhouse where we had been taken. They all teased me and said it happened because I had been to the wedding, but I hadn't, and was quite sober. They pulled the car out in twenty minutes, but they were so hearty that they damaged the steering much more than the fall into the duck pond had done!

They retrieved all our luggage, which was saturated, and the farmer found my tools. There were about three dozen because I had built up a useful tool kit.

They were wonderful, those people. They weren't well off, but they looked after us. The wife was a very ample person, and I had to pin her clothes round myself. The husband was a small man, and my father was a big man, so he had to sit without a jacket in front of the fire, in his shirt sleeves and waistcoat.'

(Which was more comfortable than the situation of the yokel who heaved a rock at Mr Edge!)

When Motoring Was Fun

An accident in the lane near St Ervan, Cornwall, in about 1937. A visitor has misjudged the width of the lane and pushed William Lobb's car into the hedge.

They then got out their Christmas things, their Christmas pudding and cake to feed us, and they wouldn't take any pay for it, and they were not at all well off. Soon after we tipped into the duck pond the bakers van that had been standing there drove into Indian Queens, and spread the news, and literally in half an hour a crowd appeared carrying every sort of light, even naked candles. You saw all these lights coming down the road, it was a wonderful sight. They had never had such excitement in all their lives.

My uncle was on the County Council then, and in no time at all they'd fenced that duck pond, put up white posts and drained it.' Which was sad for the ducks, and the local population, now deprived of their excitement!

One of the most common causes of rural accidents was when visitors to the area misjudged the width of their vehicles in the narrow lanes. The photograph above shows the result of just such a mistake, and a sad coming together.

The Ford 8, which may have been quite new, has got plenty of space to pass, but has not used it, with expensive results.

Childhood events tend to stay in the memory, when what happened yesterday is a blank, and I vividly remember my father taking a party to Chagford to visit an aged relative in the little Hillman Minx in about 1948. As we toiled up a hill a large Alvis came charging down, and misjudging the

width of the road ripped along the side of out car with his front bumper. It did a lot of damage to wings and body work, and even caused a flat tyre, and what made my father so angry was that all the Alvis suffered was a slightly bent bumper!

However, not everyone got off so lightly. The owner of this 60 horsepower Napier Phaeton (ooposite) of 1910 vintage was a Mr Arthur Nalder, and this accident happened to his 36cwt vehicle at Dibberford farm, near Beaminster. As can be seen in the photograph, attempts at recovery are under way, with the erection of a shear legs to try and lift the wreckage. It is interesting to note that when the car was re-registered, presumably after the accident, it had become a Landaulette, and was a different colour. One hopes it was an improvement on the original, after all that adventure.

The presence of narrow roads and streets, and the inexperience of some drivers, meant that cars frequently collided with things at the roadside, in preference to other cars! Town and villages, built long before the motoring age, presented many challenges to the driver, and especially a driver who might be going a little fast.

In the Thatcham photograph we find that the S-bend from Chapel Street into the High Street has caught out yet another unfortunate motorist, this time driving what looks like a Model T Ford saloon, the one rather unkindly described as 'the hearse.' Here the car driver has crashed his vehicle into C.G. Brown's shop, with mutual damage. One feels

Early Days on the Open Road

A nasty overturning for a Napier car near Beaminster, Dorset, about 1919.

Not the way to go shopping, Broadway, Thatcham in Berkshire, and a Model T Ford about 1920.

that the Ford's front axle will never quite be the same again.

Even out in rural areas there could be some strange goings on. The photographs on the following pages show Marchant's Cross, up on Dartmoor, near Meavy, one of the tallest granite crosses on Dartmoor, a truly venerable stone.

However, the cross was no match for a 1930s vintage Morris car, when driven by a Mr Jury with the permission of the owner Bill Northmore. In 1937 he knocked the cross over when the brakes failed on his car.

Knowing Dartmoor as I do, and its myriad of supernatural inhabitants, I should say that the penalties for knocking over such an ancient cross would be horrific. But maybe the inhabitants of the moor were so flabbergasted at the coming of the motor car that they let the driver off with a caution!

Bill Northmore with his Morris car, after it knocked over Marchant's Cross on Dartmoor in 1937.

If driving a car along narrow winding roads was a challenge, with steep hills at intervals to keep one on ones toes, it was always worse going down than going up, then driving large lorries and other heavy vehicles was even more difficult, and you could not afford to make mistakes. The poor steamroller in the photograph on the page opposite may look worse than it really is, as apart from the front roller the rest looks to be intact, and they were built with a lot of strength, as weight only made them more effective in their work.

One of the main reasons for lorries overturning was because they had been overloaded, or the load was top heavy. There was always that temptation to squeeze a bit more on the back to save an extra trip, and those loading up in the yard were inclined to forget the forces at work once a lorry got under way and was out on the open road. A lorry that was quite stable at speed going up a straight road would be highly unstable if rounding a bend, even at a modest speed. Likewise, great forces could be brought to bear if a lorry tried to brake too quickly, including the danger of jack-knifing, when the trailer of an articulated lorry swings round at right angles to the cab unit.

In recent years the introduction of a huge number of roundabouts on our main roads has been a most effective way of sorting out the lorries that are badly loaded or being driven too fast, but the downside is that certain roads seem to be constantly blocked by overturned vehicles.

It is only fairly recently that quays and riverside roads have had safety barriers, the old-fashioned thought being that no one could be silly enough to drive their vehicle over the edge and into the water Photographs, however, tell a different story!.

A Foden chain-driven lorry in trouble on the bridge at Staverton about 1910.

Early Days on the Open Road

When a steamroller runs away the results can be most spectacular. Bideford in 1910 had not had such excitement for years!

Today, when I go on a journey, upon arrival I hop out of the car, press a key fob, the car winks at me, and the doors lock automatically.

When I started motoring, it was not like that. If you reached your journey's end, you would switch off your engine, and savour the peace for a moment or two. You would then unwind yourself from your seat, and climb stiffly out. Having loosened up a bit, you would then walk slowly round your car, peering underneath at intervals, to see what had dropped off on the journey.

My father told the story of cousin William, who about the year 1925 purchased what was for him a new car. In fact it had seen much better days. William was very proud of it, and it being a lovely spring day he decided to celebrate by taking his Aunt Ethel for a spin in the country.

William reached the old lady's cottage safely, and with great difficulty persuaded her to come for an outing. She was installed on the back seat, with a rug, and insisted on having her umbrella as it was an open car. They set off, and had gone about two miles down the bumpy country road, when she tapped William on his right shoulder. Because of the general noise, William could not hear what she was saying, but assumed she was drawing his attention to the carpet of Bluebells in the wood on their right.

'Very lovely, Auntie,' he shouted,' a real sign of spring!' And he drove on.

Presently, after a mile or so, she tapped him on the left shoulder. William assumed she was drawing his attention to the lambs gambolling in the field away to their left.

Lovely little chaps,' William shouted,' pity they will be chops so soon.'

They drove on, and after another mile Aunt hit him over the head with the handle of her umbrella. William stopped, feeling injured, and climbed out.

'Come here, William,' commanded his Aunt, pointing to the back of the car by her feet, 'Is it supposed to be like this?'

William peered into the back. All the wooden floor boards had fallen out into the road, and his Aunt's feet were dangling a couple of inches or so above the surface of the road!

The Cornhill is the centre of Ipswich, where four roads meet, and in olden days a policeman stood on duty directing the traffic. The story goes that one day he heard a very loud noise approaching along Tavern Street, and when the car in question reached the Cornhill the policeman rather imperiously stopped it. Having done so he went round to the driver's window.

'I believe sir, that you have lost your exhaust system' said the Policeman.

Even for racing drivers it is unnerving to be overtaken by your own back wheel!

'Thank you, officer, but I have not lost it,' replied the driver.

The policeman drew himself up to his full height, and raised his voice a bit.

'I have had great experience of motor cars over the years, sir' he declared, 'and I know that when a car is making the amount of noise that this car is making, then you have lost your exhaust system.'

'I beg to contradict you, officer' replied the driver, 'but I have not lost my exhaust system. It is lying on the back seat!'

The photograph above is a reminder of something that happened to many early motorists at one time or another. Perhaps the most arresting detail here is the expression on the driver's face. In this instance his back axle had actually broken, so the car would have lurched down on to the road, giving instant warning that all was not well behind.

In my brother's case, he was gently driving along in his 1933 Austin 7, when he was overtaken by a stray wheel. The car proceeded quite normally, and Nick said it was some moments before he realised it was his own wheel. He was an experienced driver, and brought the car to a stop very gently, so that it was not until he actually stopped moving that the rear of the car with the missing wheel subsided on to its brake drum. Nick was able to get out, retrieve his errant wheel, jack up the car and put it back on using a nut from each of the other wheels, and proceed on his journey. Cost of the misfortune was four wheel nuts, but the benefit was a lesson in checking the nuts were all tight every so often!

My friend Colin's father owned a Morgan 3-wheeler, a car mentioned in the last chapter, which was his pride and joy. One day the family set off from Manningtree to go to Harwich, in Essex, along a road which was a bit of a switchback. Coming to the top of a hill, the driver put his foot down, as one did, to get up maximum speed going down hill in order to tackle the hill ahead.

As the little car reached the bottom of the hill, at speed, there was a terrible lurch and crunch at the front, the offside of the car dropped on to the road, and the front wheel took off on its own up the next hill! Colin declares it was amazing how quickly his father reacted to this disaster. He was out of the open car within a second of it coming to rest, and set off after the wheel.

The wheel, however, had a good start, and near the top of the hill it came to a stop, and began to roll back, retracing its steps. Colin's father looked up and saw his wheel heading for him at increasing speed.

He just had time to jump to one side to avoid being run over, and could then only stand and watch as the wheel narrowly missed the wrecked car containing his family, and rolled up the hill opposite, finally coming to rest in the ditch.

Colin's father delighted in tinkering with his cars, and on another occasion, with a different car, he decided that the brakes needed attention. He drained all the brake fluid out, disconnected the brake pipes, and then discovered that he needed a different tool, so retired into the garage to look for it. At that point Colin's mother, who was an impulsive lady, decided that as she had finished her housework early, she would pop up and see her mother, so she grabbed Colin, rushed out, couldn't see her husband anywhere, so she jumped into the car and set off out of the drive.

Early Days on the Open Road

Father came out of the garage just in time to see the car disappear round the corner into the road, and knew at once that it had no brakes at all! They got as far as the first corner, where fortunately a friendly bank stopped further hair raising progress!

In those days we were most enthusiastic about adorning our cars with extra badges, mirrors and lights, and these would often fall off on a journey and not be missed until later. There was never any point in going back to look for things in miles of ditches along the route.

Larger items, however, would usually let you know they had come adrift or fallen off. We had rather makeshift luggage carriers to fix on the back of cars which had no boot, and these could tip up, causing a suitcase or trunk to scatter its contents in the road behind. One friend remembers that in his case it was his mother-in-law's suitcase, and she was not at all amused at having all her undergarments scattered down the road in the public gaze!

We also carried a lot on luggage racks on our car roofs, which must have been a lot stronger than they are today! Sometimes items would come loose in the wind, and fly away in the vehicles slipstream. At other times there would be a horrible scraping noise on the roof, followed by a crash, as the whole thing came adrift from its moorings, and fell onto the road behind, to be run over by the lorry that had been closely following you!

Trams could pose particular problems, partly because they obviously had to keep to their tracks, and partly because motorists sometimes forget this simple fact. I have seen somewhere a photograph of two trams at a standstill, with the remains of a very squashed car between them.

I can't help wondering whether that was the inspiration for a lovely cartoon by Russell Brockbank, whose motoring cartoons are legendary. This one shows two trams, with a car very firmly stuck between them. The driver of one tram, and the conductor of the other, are showing very plainly that they are not amused by what has happened. Meanwhile the driver of the car, who seems to have ended up with his head sticking out of the fabric roof, is looking very cheerful, and saying;

'Ah well, nothing venture, nothing win!'

Quite how this tram in the photograph below came to capsize is a bit of a mystery, and it must have been a very upsetting experience for the passengers, and especially those on the upper deck.

I don't feel I can end this chapter without a reference to the fact that with increasing traffic congestion, ever more frustration and hugely greater speeds, accidents today are nothing to smile about, and frequently the source of pain and tragedy.

This tram overturned at the junction of Park Lane and Ruskin Road, Carshalton, on 1 April 1907.

When Motoring Was Fun

Nicky Tregear was driving Zacky Nicholas' lorry in Sennen, Cornwall, in the 1920s when he took this wrong turning. Willing helpers, some seen here, helped to recover the precariously balanced vehicle.

Sadly, accidents have always drawn a crowd, as the photograph over the page reminds us. Today, on our busy motorways and main roads, human nature hasn't changed, and many a bad situation is made worse by motorists in the unaffected carriageway jamming on their brakes so as to get a good look at the accident scene. We have all been 'gawpers', but the result of such slowing down is often to cause fresh accidents!

Quite how the lorry in the photograph above ended up where it did is also a mystery, but we are told that fortunately it was on its way to the quarry to pick up a load of building stone, so was unladen. Otherwise recovering it from such a position would have been very difficult. This is a final instance of something which was not very funny at the time, but which caused a lot of local excitement, and provided a good story to tell the family or the regulars in the pub.

In retrospect, we seem to be able to see the funny side of things when our beloved Transports of Delight come to grief, and while we may be temporally shattered, clinging to a broken headlight as our vehicle is towed away, our sense of perspective is usually restored by a stiff whisky, and a chance to explain to a rather bored audience that given this or that circumstance the accident couldn't possibly have been our fault!

Chapter 10

CARS FOR ALL OCCASIONS

All types of motor transport vie for their place in the road against pedestrians, and horse-drawn transport, London c.1923. Along the centre of Victoria Street a line of taxi cabs wait for hire.

Just as the horse-drawn chariot of Boadicea and the Romans eventually gave way to the armoured car and the tank, so did the many specialised horse-drawn carriages and carts evolve into motor vehicles of many varieties.

I am not sure whether the horse-drawn tumbrel was the direct forerunner of the taxi. The taxi was certainly not confined to one way journeys with very reluctant fares on the way to meet Madame Guillotine! London and other large cities had always had their fleets of passenger vehicles for hire, and in London these were known as Hansom or Hackney cabs. The latter name lived on, as the London taxis which followed the demise of the horse-drawn vehicles had a plate on the back saying 'Hackney Carriage. Licensed to carry 5 persons.'

Many of the pre-war London taxis were supplied by Austin and Morris, with special coach built bodies. The design was very practical. Three passengers could sit comfortably across the back seat, facing forward, and another two passengers could sit on folding seats that faced the rear. The driver had his own compartment, and the space beside him was for luggage, and could hold a good deal. There was also a reasonable boot. The whole vehicle was kept as short as possible to aid parking and manoeuvrability, and a modification in steering design gave it a remarkably small turning circle. One had to keep on one's toes, driving in London, because a London taxi driver spotting a potential fare on the opposite side of the street would execute an immediate U turn to grab the passenger before another taxi spotted him!

London taxi drivers were required to know the whole of London's geography, and to pass a test on it, and they would explore on bicycles, map in hand, until they knew all the roads they might be required to visit. Perhaps this accounts for the taxi driver's attitude to other motorists who ventured on to the London streets, and explains why we were so pleased to see them put to flight by my mother driving the Land Rover with her usual exuberance!

When Motoring Was Fun

Mr Porter of Stithians driving his taxi in the 1920s with a full load of local people.

One must admit that the London taxis maintained a very high standard in every respect during the period before the mini-cab, and a consequent free-for-all which ensued. Drivers were courteous and helpful, perhaps in expectation of a tip! and they certainly knew their way around the capital, though sometimes indulging in diversions down little known routes either to avoid a traffic jam, or add a bit more on to the reading on their meter!

In country districts, such as my native Devon, the situation was very different. In the towns there would have been a few taxi companies, but our nearest was run by the Harris family who operated the garage in nearby Ipplepen. The family consisted of a sister, Miss Harris, who did the accounts and acted as secretary, and probably ran the whole show, if the truth was known. Then there were three brothers, Bill, Reg and Alf, and a nephew, Douglas, who had been a Royal Air Force ground staff member through the war, and was far and away the best mechanic for miles around.

The family ran two large Austin 18s, which were used as limousines for weddings and funerals, and also as taxis. If you asked for a taxi to meet you at the station, or to come to your house, and the car arrived with plenty of time to spare, you could be certain it was being driven by Bill or Reg. These two brothers never hurried, enjoyed a bit of a chat about the weather, the crops or family matters, and they both drove with great care and decorum

through the winding narrow lanes.

If the taxi arrived on time, it was probably in the hands of Alf. Alf moved faster than his brothers, and had less inclination to conversation. He also drove the old cars a good deal faster. If the taxi arrived late, it would be Douglas at the wheel, and he would explain briefly that he had been in the middle of a ticklish engineering challenge when called away. He would then show you just how fast the old Austin could go when there was a train to catch at Newton Abbot. To be fair, I only remember it being Douglas driving on a couple of occasions, but for some reason they have remained firmly imprinted on my memory!

During and after the war, this taxi service, which was very reasonably priced, was a godsend to us, partly because of the difficulty of getting petrol, and partly because of the number of family members who could be squeezed into the old but spacious cars. I can still hear Reg, who was the friendliest of the quartet, saying in his soft Devon brogue 'Room for another little one over here, Captain Tyler.' I imagine that as the Harris family were operating both a garage and a taxi service they had some special access to supplies of precious petrol.

The story of Murdoch Mackay of Bakewell, in the Peak District, gives us an insight into the sort of business that came into being. A Scot from Edinburgh, Murdoch came south to work as a forester on the Chatsworth Estate about 1910. At the out-

Murdoch Mackay standing beside his 1920s taxis in Bakewell. The car on the left did the Sheffield run, the other did local services.

break of war in 1914 he returned North to enlist in the Cameron Highlanders, and then, having survived the conflict, returned to Bakewell and became first a lorry driver, and then drove the town's fire engine and the ambulance. In 1919 he purchased his first vehicle, a Maudsley, and started his taxi service. In the 1920s he built up a fleet of vehicles, operating a bus service as well, and it was his boast that he originated the first 'Mystery Tours' at half a crown (12½ pence) a head! In the 1930s he even purchased a 1926 Rolls-Royce which was used for wedding and funeral occasions, and at other times for special outings as far afield as Blackpool!

We have touched on weddings and funerals, and here the car came to play a large part. Undertakers would keep their own fleet of cars, including a hearse, preferably with matching registration numbers, and of the same make and model. The hearse was designed so that it could carry two coffins at once, one above, and on display, and one tucked in underneath out of sight. This not only saved extra journeys, but if a coffin had to be picked up from a distance, it could be slipped in underneath, and the hearse could bowl along at sixty miles per hour without causing offence to passers by, who thought it was empty!

A very grand 1948 Daimler motor hearse now restored and on show in the Ipswich Transport Museum. It carried two coffins.

If it was actually on the way to a funeral, it could be pulled off the road into a quiet and secluded lay-by, the coffin moved up on top, and flowers added, and then the assistants could dress up, and the now very dignified vehicle could proceed on its way at a decorous twenty miles per hour.

I used to chat to the drivers of hearses on occasions, and they were cheerful folk, and very good drivers. They did, however, have two great fears. One was breaking down on the way to a funeral, and the other, even worse, was being involved in an accident in a similar situation.

When Motoring Was Fun

Two wedding cars at Uplyme in Dorset in 1922, the one on the right a Model T Ford.

Sadly, in some circumstances, people feel the need to have a funeral that is as ostentatious as possible, aware that their neighbours will all be watching them. It is understandably a time when grief often clouds judgement, and so a vast Rolls-Royce hearse if followed by five or six similar limousines, and the ultimate bill is pretty horrific.

The same can apply, in a different way, to weddings. A wedding is seen as 'the brides special day' and therefore no expense can be spared to enable her to have everything she desires, including a huge posh shiny car to carry her to the church.

Mr and Mrs Charlie Stocker were the first couple to go by car to Uplyme Church for their wedding. The scene is set outside Loom Cottage, the home of the Fishers, Mrs Stocker's family, for five generations. The dresses and white ribbons on the car have not changed a lot down the years!

A number of factors have crept in to change the situation over the years, however. First, in many cases this is not the only 'big day' that the bride may enjoy during her lifetime, - or the bridegroom too, for that matter. Second, while a church often makes a lovely setting for a grand wedding car, a crowded street outside a registry office does not have the same ambience. Then as everything connected with weddings began to get hideously expensive, many couples looked for ways to cut the expense, and called upon Uncle Richard who drove a nice Jaguar. Finally, a lot of couples decided they wanted to do something different, something to make the day special to themselves. Some reverted to a horse and carriage, or even a pony trap. Excellent unless you are planning a long journey to an airport to go on your honeymoon! Others, eager to capture the nostalgic feeling, opted for a vintage car, and these could easily be found either by contacting a Vintage Vehicle Club, or looking for a car hire company that specialised in vintage cars. I once had the opportunity while my car was being repaired to look round some old battery chicken houses that had been converted. Inside them I found twelve Rolls-Royces, dating between 1928 and 1956, and all gleaming with polish and attired with white ribbons ready for wedding duty.

Weddings could often be a little hair raising, and I remember one in particular when we found just as the bride was about to arrive that we were missing a rather important ingredient for the ceremony in the person of the bridegroom!

The church was located up a short cul-de-sac off the main road, so an usher was hastily dispatched to stop the bride arriving, and send her car round the block to pass the time. When she arrived back again a few minutes later, having cruised down the nearby village street, we still had no bridegroom, so she was waved away and did the circuit again. By this time onlookers in the village were getting both bewildered and amused. Fortunately at that point

Early Days on the Open Road

Billy Crane, who organised motorised weddings in Sculthorpe, Norfolk, between 1929 and 1955 holds the door open for bride Gwen Lingwood and her father. The car may be a large Austin.

Postbridge church outing on Dartmoor in the early 1930s, with the help of a large Austin 18.

her intended arrived, his car had broken down, and he had to hitch a lift. His bride looked highly relieved when on the third attempt she was allowed to approach the church, and even more relieved when told that her groom was inside waiting for her, if a little breathless!

Another bride-to-be came to visit me, and at once spotted Delilah, my little Austin 7 box saloon, parked in the front drive (see page 37). She at once decided that this was to be her wedding car, and nothing I could say would dissuade her.

It was fortunate that we had a rehearsal, so that we could check that it was physically possible to get the three of us into the car. I am not exactly a lightweight, but the bride's father made me seem so, and the bride herself, a lovely lass, was also well built! We got her on to the back seat with some difficulty, and she had to sit sideways, with a leg up on the seat. Her father and I had to coincide the shutting of the doors, otherwise one or other of us would have been shot out sideways! In the event it was more than cosy, and I had great difficulty changing the gears.

However, Delilah did discover one great advantage for us, and that was that she was so small she could creep through the lych gate, and down the yew-lined path to the church door. In the event it was a lovely day full of sunshine, the bride's dress survived the journey intact, and the whole thing was voted a great success!

While cars of all descriptions could play their parts in weddings and funerals, the car could also be pressed into service for outings. At a school I attended on the edge of Dartmoor, catering for boys aged 8 to 13, the headmaster, Mr Wedd, drove a 1939 Morris 8 series E, which was christened Titch.

One of the regular events on the school calendar were sports matches played away at other schools, usually with eleven players in the team, and Mr Wedd would regularly get a whole team into Titch, complete with their equipment if it was a cricket match. That was really a wonderful little car!

In the picture of the Postbridge Church outing in the 1930s, we appear to have three adults, one male, the driver perhaps, and two female, and nine children, two of them pretty large. They appear to be still on Dartmoor, so perhaps had not driven all that far for the treat. Is it the drivers wife still standing in the car, with her head out of the sun roof? How the children would have enjoyed travelling like that, it reminds me of my army days, driving in convoy with my head out of the roof hatch on the Matador.

My mother organised children's trips in our village, notably for the Sunday School children to pick primroses for Mothering Sunday. I can remember some very full cars, but have no record of how many children she managed to squash in. It was the days before seat belts, of course, and the journeys were very short and local.

In the world of medicine we had two vehicles that appeared in the country districts. One, a quite frequent visitor, would be the doctor's car. It did not have 'Doctor' written on it, or anything like that, but we all knew it.

The other vehicle which could appear on rare occasions, and always caused quite a stir, was the local ambulance. In our case this would have come from one of the towns six or seven miles away, so its arrival meant someone was really ill. Many of the early ambulances were run by the St John's Ambulance Brigade, and were not the white vehicles that appeared after the Second World War.

A 1926 Bullnose Morris, known by all as 'The Doctors Coupe', pictured at Bridestowe, Devon.

In the photograph below we see the first ambulance in Seaton, which was created from a Chrysler car donated by Dr James, and then converted by A. Dowell and Sons, coachbuilders in Exeter. It must have been a pretty robust car to cope with the heavy body fitted to it. Certainly it was the pride and joy of the local St John Ambulance men, and doubtless gave good service over very many years, being lovingly cared for and carefully serviced and maintained.

In the early years Ambulances were rather like lifeboats, individually attached to a particular town, and often supported by public subscription. The vehicles themselves, as we have seen, differed a lot in origin and design. The one thing they had in common was that they saved lives, and the ringing of a distant ambulance bell brought a sense of hope and relief to those suffering, or watching over a patient. The ambulance crews also had a great deal of expe-

rience, and a lot of medical knowledge picked up over the years, so often were able to give vital first aid until a patient could be attended to in hospital.

Later ambulances were more standard, purpose-built vehicles, with larger bodies on a van or small lorry chassis. There were exceptions, and for some time many ambulances were put on larger Daimler car chassis.

The other vehicle which rang its bell and caused a huge sense of relief in all communities was the fire engine. The old horse-drawn engines, some with steam-operated pumps, gave way to motor vehicles in the early twentieth century and these engines, with the capacity to carry a team of firemen as well as water and long ladders were much more effective vehicles than anything that had preceded them. This was just as well, because buildings were getting ever larger, and materials in use became highly inflammable in some cases.

Once again fire engines saved lives, and as the vehicles became faster they could reach the scene of a fire much more quickly, when seconds often made a difference. The fire brigade was rightly seen as most important, and nationally funded. Firemen were on duty twenty-four hours a day, and naturally cared for their most important vehicles, keeping them at the peak of efficiency. There was no point receiving an urgent summons to a fire if you then found that your fire engine would not start!

Firemen also needed to have good local knowledge. In country areas hay and straw ricks could overheat and catch fire, and these could easily be in very remote locations.

The commissioning of the new ambulance in Seaton, Devon, in 1938.

Early Days on the Open Road

The fire engine at Highfield Avenue, Brundall, Norfolk, seen in all its splendour in about 1938.

I remember one very hot summer's day sitting looking out across the valley in front of our home, and watching two small boys from the village wander across the field and disappear behind the newly built hay stack half a mile away. After a minute or two they reappeared, moving much faster, and headed back the way they had come, looking over their shoulders at intervals. Soon we noticed a thin column of smoke going up into the air from behind the stack, and my father rushed indoors to the telephone. Describing the exact whereabouts of the burning stack was not easy, even for a soldier with a good grasp of map reading. However, the fire engine found the correct gate, and thanks to the dry weather was able to get up across the field to the stack, which by that time was completely engulfed in flames.

A second phone call to the village policeman, a good friend, meant that the two culprits were picked up in the village square shortly afterwards, having foolishly dallied to boast to friends of what they had done!

The fire engines of the period did not have four-wheel drive, but in the hands of a skilled driver they could do very well across country if they had to. The early fire engines only had room for two or three men to travel in the cab, and the other members of the crew sat on seats that faced outwards at the back of the vehicle, and there being no seat belts or anything like that they had to hold on to whatever was handy. Due to the skill of drivers, and

the courtesy of other road users when they saw a fire engine coming, I never heard of a member of the crew being thrown off, but I suppose it must have happened.

The arrival of the car also made it much easier for those in positions of importance to visit much further afield, and especially in rural areas. We have seen how election candidates used cars for campaigning activity, something which has continued more noisily ever since.

For the Church, the use of cars meant that dignitaries could be driven to visit parishes in far flung parts of the diocese. Here the Dean of Exeter, resplendent in gaiters, and not perhaps in the first flush of youth, appears to be holding on to the car

Dean Gamble from Exeter Cathedral pays a visit to High Bickington, Devon, in about 1928.

When Motoring Was Fun

door for support, after perhaps a rather rough journey, or else a generous glass or two of port. The car might even be a Rolls-Royce, for Deans had considerable incomes at that period.

Being able to provide your church dignitaries with a car and driver also had other advantages.

Bishop Cecil of Exeter was a lovely man but notoriously forgetful, and was always helping himself to the wrong bicycle outside the cathedral because he could never remember what his own looked like. (The Chapter eventually painted his cycle all the colours of the rainbow in an effort to assist the bishop's memory, but even that did not always work!)

On one occasion the bishop was travelling west from Exeter via the Great Western Railway, and was visited by the ticket inspector. In vain the bishop hunted through his many pockets. His ticket was nowhere to be found.

'Now don't you worry, My Lord,' said the inspector, even more embarrassed than the bishop. 'We all know your Lordship. It doesn't matter if you can't find your ticket.'

'Of course it matters,' replied the bishop testily. 'Without that ticket I have no idea where I am supposed to be going to!'

With the arrival of the car the problem was solved, and the bishop could be confidently placed in the hands of a good driver who would guarantee to get him to the right place at the right time!

Cars could also be adapted for other special activities, and one of these was the local carnival. Carnival processions go back many years, and horse drawn wagons, appropriately decorated, were the order of the day. With the coming of the motor vehicle there was scope for further improvisation and inventiveness, with the result that bigger and better floats were always appearing as groups sought to out do each other year by year.

The couple from Bampton in Devon are driving what almost looks to be a car built specially for the occasion! I must confess I have not been able to identify it.

Harry Pengelly's Lorry becomes a transport of delight for children at the Lydford Carnival, celebrating King George V's Silver Jubilee in 1935.

Sophie Burston and Brendon Tayler as Darby and Joan in the Bampton Carnival in 1949.

Queen Elizabeth the Queen Mother arrives at St Mawes in 1969 in a royal Daimler.

Larger vehicles, such as the lorry at Lydford Carnival, could transport much larger numbers of carnival competitors, and gave much scope for decoration.

Finally, there were those very special occasions indeed when royalty paid a visit to a town or village, and although the royal train continued in use, the royal cars took over more of these duties often in conjunction with the train. For most of this time the Royal family continued to use Daimlers, and it was perhaps when Daimler ceased to be a British company that the decision was taken to use Rolls-Royce cars. Now that Rolls-Royce cars is no longer a British company there must be a bit of a problem, but I doubt we shall see them arriving in Morgans!

Chapter 11

FIRST CARS AND LEARNING TO DRIVE

'High Calamity', with three reluctant passengers, ready for take off, Elm Park, Devon, 1949. A grandmother looks on eagerly!

I suppose that in a way it all starts in the pram. That feeling of drifting effortlessly through town or country, sitting in great comfort, propelled in a transport of delight that at once offers a splendid view of the passing scenery, and at the same time rests those tired little legs!

In my case I was fortunate that at the moment I came along my older twin brothers had just about worn out their pram. I therefore was endowed with a new pram, and in due course got my hands on the old one, which I christened 'High Calamity.' At home in Devon we had a steep bank leading down to a large flat lawn, ideal for testing vehicles, and High Calamity hurtled down the bank in a variety of guises.

At first the problem of propulsion occupied me, and having acquired a surplus seven pound biscuit tin, I installed it, and then carefully arranged a number of hollow hogweed stems inside. I felt that given the right formula it would go. It didn't! An older brother persuaded me that if I set fire to it, the desired result would occur. We tried, and were left with no signs of movement, but a small pile of ash where the dry hogweed stems had burnt magnificently!

I soon realised the value of the long hill in the lane outside the house, which made a motor unnecessary, but which did require steering, as there were two sharp corners. High Calamity was given a rebuild, with a lengthened chassis, wooden front wheel blocks and track rod, and metal stub axles and king pins taken from another derelict pram. For a steering column I had the barrel of a discarded .410 shotgun, with a pram wheel for steering wheel. Brakes did not really feature at all, and the bonnet was an old metal fireguard.

All in all it worked pretty well, and gave hours of pleasure. There was, however, always a risk to give a spice of adventure. The lane was spattered with pot holes of varying sizes, and if a front wheel

Early Days on the Open Road

A young Michael Godfrey from Wolverhampton in his pedal car c.1954.

Charioteers at Leigh Sinton, Worcestershire, in the 1980s.

dropped into even the smallest of these the shock to the system could cause partial disintegration of the steering assembly, and a rapid dive into the ditch beside the road. In fact that happened just after the photo opposite was taken, but was not captured on camera as the photographer was laughing too much!

Many years later, when I had children of my own, I got a craftsman to weld me a couple of chassis, with better steering and pedal driven chain to the back wheels, and I made interchangeable bodies for them, as I had noticed how limited the average child's pedal car seemed to be. These proved very popular, and now need re-furbishing for grandchildren!

I have watched children driving such cars a good deal, and I am convinced that they learn control of the car, including reversing and parking, and even how to achieve a neat three point turn.

As a child we looked with a good deal of longing at the Triang and other pedal cars of the day, that were far too expensive to be considered. I remember one modelled on the Austin A40 Devon which I would have given almost anything to possess.

If you had enough money there were obviously some very exciting cars you could buy, and I remember an exhibition at the National Motor Museum at Beaulieu which included a battery-driven 4½ litre Bentley. However, I have never seen or heard of the children's car shown in the following picture, and I wonder whether it really did

A beautifully made child's car takes to the streets in Addiscombe, in the 1930s.

When Motoring Was Fun

The Wilesmith family of Leigh. Worcestershire, with a most exciting and superior children's car c.1938.

This children's car is self starting, and capable of 16mph but we do not know details of the engine!

work? According to the description, it had forward and reverse gears, and rather comfortingly for parents, a brake! We are not told what speeds it attained, or, more important, how far it would go before it needed pumping up again, but at least that provided warming exercise on a cold day.

Finally, after many miles of driving all sorts of vehicles, including prams, as a child, the moment comes when we are let loose on the road, with a 'L' plate on the back of the car. Many, like myself, have already had 'off road' driving practice, sometimes on a tractor, so it is not such a new experience, and I always taught my pupils the basics of car control somewhere other than on the open road, or worse still a crowded street! In those days we were fortu-

nate to have abandoned airfields which were ideal places to start out on a driving career.

Driving tuition varied a lot down the years. My mother remembers 'My father was very clever. In 1921, when he bought our first car, he arranged for a mechanic from Skeltons Garage to come with it and stay for a week to teach me to drive and maintain the car.' That was the extent of my mother's tuition, and she never had to pass a driving test. She taught most of the family to drive, as well as other friends, and she finally gave up when she was about ninety four. I have no idea how many hundreds of thousands of miles she must have driven in those seventy four years.

The subject of driving tuition and the dreaded driving test have always been a great source of humour, and many of Brockbank's and Thelwell's cartoons cover the subject in all its many possibilities and disasters!

As traffic congestion and speed have increased over the years, so have the number and seriousness of accidents. The powers that be in the Department of Transport have reacted to this by introducing more and more regulations, strewing the roads with more and more signs, and making the driving test ever more tough and complicated.

In the days we are considering, when you taught someone to drive, you had two aims. The first was to give them confidence in the control of the car,

This unique miniature Atco car was designed to train drivers in the late1930s, and is now in the Ipswich Transport Museum.

and in tackling the circumstances they would meet out on the open road. Learning to steer, brake and change gear were all part of this. The second aim was much more difficult. It involved enabling the person to develop a correct judgement with regard to distance and speed. In the days before miles and miles of dual carriageways, overtaking was a very important part of driving, and many accidents occurred, and still do occur, because the overtaking car does not make a correct judgement of the relative distances and speeds of other vehicles. Many other accidents occur because of cornering at the wrong speed for the road conditions or the severity of the corner.

The only way in my view to help someone develop this essential judgement was to let them spend many hours behind the wheel, driving in 'open road' conditions, rather than pottering round cul-de-sacs on a housing estate, learning very little and getting in everyone's way!

Finally came the dreaded driving test, which in my day lasted an hour, and included time for checking licences and forms, and also answering questions based on the Highway Code.

I was most anxious to get my licence in the school summer holidays, which lasted seven weeks. You could not take your test in less than three weeks after your seventeenth birthday, and then must allow four weeks before you took another test, if you failed the first one. I had actually been driving after a fashion since the age of thirteen, being somewhat obsessed with cars, so booked the first test for three weeks after my birthday, and took it in the family Land Rover, with a small chalk mark on the rear tailboard to help me when reversing into a parking space!

I failed. The examiner informed me that I did not use my mirrors enough, I had three, one inside, and two on the front of the wings. Four weeks later

PUMPING UP.

ON THE ROAD.

This little car is driven by air. Its speed is controlled by a throttle and it has one lever for brake and one for reverse.

A child's car that the child pumps up and then drives away, c.1935.

another very delightful examiner let me drive him round for fifteen minutes, and then we pulled into a quiet road and chatted about cricket, of which he was a great fan, for half an hour. I remember it was a lovely warm sunny day, and I remember the joy of removing the 'L' plates from the car and driving my mother home.

It is very sad that after all that has been done to improve tuition and testing, a hugely disproportionate number of accidents occur involving young male drivers who have only been driving a year or two.

Passing one's driving test, and being able to afford a car, were always two quite different things, even though petrol was about ninety-five pence for four gallons!

For many young people the cost of even a second hand car would take most of their savings, in my case the huge sum of £75 in 1956. The car was twenty-one years old, a Morris 8 Tourer (see page 38) bought from a friend of my father, who also lived in the village. However, it filled me with a huge sense of pride, and I would spend many

Mother and daughter pose with an newly acquired car at Pimperne in Dorset, c.1920.

hours out in the garage cosseting it. I actually bought it a few months before my birthday, so couldn't drive it out on the road. My eldest son did the same thing twenty-eight years later when he bought his Riley RME.

It goes without saying that those old cars had their own individual personalities, and their character was usually not apparent on first meeting.

In the photograph above you can see the proud owners revelling in the occasion. Their son has brought his new convertible down to show it off to the family. It is a lovely sunny day, and soon he will take his sister out for a spin, with the hood down, and give her a motoring experience the like of which she has never known before, while she can wave in proud delight to those by the roadside she

happens to recognise. Given that the weather looks fine, and, more importantly, that the car is new, or only just secondhand, the expedition should be a highly successful one.

However, as I have hinted, it was not necessarily so! If, as was usually the case, you bought your car from a garage, then you would find that garages varied enormously. My father always bought his cars from the same dealer in nearby Totnes, and that way he knew them, and they knew him, and knew that he would be back! They were very good, and stood by their cars, so that for example when we had problems with a new Jowett Javelin, which had a habit of breaking a half shaft every so often, the garage in Totnes lent us a Vauxhall Velox as a courtesy car to tide us over while the Javelin was fixed. I can remember it well, as I was driving by then, and it drove rather like a badly sprung feather bed, rolling alarmingly round the corners; or perhaps that was just my bad driving!

May Harvey, postmistress at Widecombe-in-the-Moor on Dartmoor, with her new Austin, c.1930.

Early Days on the Open Road

Colin and Margery Sampford of Thorley, with their first car, a Morris Minor, in the 1960s.

Jim Morton of Thorley poses with his sister, and new Austin Somerset in the early 1950s.

In the picture below all ladies present are dressed with due modesty, while taking account of current fashions! It is a pity that there are so many people in the group that one can scarcely see anything of the car but three wheels. One just hopes that they did not all demand a ride at the same time, for that would probably have resulted in nothing more that a cartload of wreckage to be taken back to London!

Even as late as the 1960s buying one's first car could be a big investment, and so there was always a strong temptation to get a bargain! For some reason the secondhand car dealer has acquired a distinctive reputation over the years, and not really a very flattering one as far as the motorist has been concerned! We have already seen with the adventures of Mr Sprocket that car salesmen could be just a little devious in the pursuit of their commission!

The secondhand car dealer faced a more difficult task, but was always ready to rise to the challenge when opportunity presented itself. He knew that

Sidney and Augustus Greenwood-Penny arrive in Devon at High Bickington from London to show off their first car, about 1900.

When Motoring Was Fun

Ted Gosling of Seaton, Devon, with the 1928 Singer 8 which he purchased for a bargain £4 in 1956.

first impressions count for a great deal, so he had at his disposal a vast armoury of fillers and polishes, with every shade of paint, that could transform the look of a car in the sale room or on the forecourt.

The second priority was the inside, for the chances were that the prospective owner's wife would wish to try out the car for comfort. It was therefore important that when she settled herself into the front passenger seat a stray spring did not pierce her generous posterior. She would also examine the shine on the imitation leather seats, notice any recent stitching if it were not well camouflaged, and run her finger over the dashboard looking for dust, as she was wont to do at home.

But the biggest challenge the secondhand car salesman faced was with the new owner himself, who might often take a perverse interest in the mechanical health of his prospective car. The salesman knew quite well that there were one or two minor mechanical imperfections attached to the vehicle, which he would rather gloss over, or else feign complete ignorance concerning their presence.

Here salesmen divided into two camps. Those who flung open the bonnet, revealing a newly cleaned engine, and hoped that the smell of leaking petrol, or intermittent drip of oil would not be noticed. And then those who tried to keep the bonnet shut if at all possible, drawing attention instead to the disputable fact that the tyres were still good for a tidy few miles yet!

But every salesman faced the ultimate challenge. It was highly likely that the new owner-to-be would insist that the engine was started, and would then require a short demonstration test drive. It was therefore fairly essential that the car would do three things from a mechanical point of view. First, start up; second, cover half a mile under it's own power; third, convey the new owner and his family, if present, at least a couple of miles up the road before it broke down. Failure on any of these three was likely to jeopardise a sale.

Of course, there were tricks of the trade. The noise a gearbox made, especially in the lower gears, was a fairly good guide to its health, but worrying noises could be much reduced by the addition of a quantity of sawdust to the gearbox oil! As far as the engine was concerned, the use of the heaviest engine oil might considerably reduce that telltale cloud of blue smoke when the car was started up which indicated to most people that the pistons needed urgent attention.

Likewise, the application of liberal quantities of the thickest grease available could reduce a lot of worrying rattling noises, and make the king pins almost seem acceptable!

And so the game was played. It has to be said that within certain limits you got what you paid for. In the previous picture we see Ted Gosling of Seaton with his £4 bargain. To be fair, Ted would be the first to accept that his new car was in fact twenty eight years old, so not in the first flush of youth, though he would quickly add 'They really made them to last in those good old days!'

It also has to be pointed out that despite Ted's look of smug triumph, and the fact that the car

Early Days on the Open Road

The start of a restoration project in the late 1960s on a 1938 Morris 8 Tourer, bought for the princely sum of £12.

Mr H.A.Good, of Seaton, with the Morris Cowley which cost him 6d!

does seem on first inspection to be all present, there is a slightly worrying rope leading from the front of the car, past Ted's feet, and off stage left. Could it possibly be that there is another car attached to the unseen end of the rope? And could we thus infer that Ted's new purchase is not to be described, even by a hopeful seller, as a 'runner.'

Well, it only cost £4 so what do you expect? And I guess Ted knew what he was buying, and got it going in a few days, largely by the work of his own hands!

Mr Good, of Seaton, pictured left, did one better. He acquired his car for sixpence at the local Fete held at Bicton. And no sign of a tow rope, either!

Of course, when it came to selling your dear old car, it was a case of the gamekeeper turned poacher! Many people couldn't face the trauma of the parting, so heartlessly turned the old car in at the garage in part exchange for the shiny new model.

But for those with the courage, all the tricks of the trade came to mind. The car was cleaned as never before. Paint scratches were carefully touched up. Little jobs that had been hanging about for months were tackled. The nest of mice was evicted from beside the spare tyre. Even the jack was carefully tested and oiled.

Finally the old owner psyched himself up for the dramatic performance of his life, begging all and sundry to believe that really nothing but the cruellest necessity would part him from his beloved car. It was noticeable, however, that having achieved a sale, he had a broad grin on his face as he stuffed the cash into his trouser pocket!

Chapter 12

MAKING AND MENDING THE ROADS

The old toll gate, Dulwich, with a Wolseley 11/22hp Tourer in the 1920s.

For the earliest travellers, the only transport of delight they possessed was their two feet, so they tended to follow 'roads' which ran along the ridges of hills, avoided swampy ground, thick forests and bogs, and forded rivers where they were as shallow as possible. Many journeys were undertaken for religious reasons, which is why many of these old routes converge on Stonehenge. On the way they could wind around a good deal, avoiding obstacles.

The Romans built roads for military purposes. Their roads were required so that an army might move from one place to another in the minimum of time and with the minimum of effort. They went for two qualities, a straight road and a durable one. Their surveyors, using an instrument called a Groma, ensured that the road was as straight as possible, and then their engineers built it. On a good clay soil they would lay flints, then a layer of rammed chalk. On top of this was gravel, then another layer of rammed chalk. Finally another layer of gravel was laid, and into this were bedded stone slabs, laid like a jigsaw puzzle. In some areas where flints predominated, the construction would be mainly of chalk and flints. The road would be cam-bered, so that the rain would run off, and would have gutters along each side. These were the first real roads, found throughout the Roman Empire, and they were to last for many centuries.

After the departure of the Romans, there followed many centuries of neglect for the roads. The problem was that no-one was responsible for their upkeep, and no money was made available.

It took a great national fright to begin a remedy for the situation. In 1745, General Wade and his army were weather bound at Newcastle-upon-Tyne, unable to move, and Bonnie Prince Charlie and his Scots army slipped past them and marched as far south as Derby. London seemed to be at his mercy, and it was only dissent within his ranks which caused him to retreat back to Scotland.

This narrow escape made the government realise that good roads were essential for national security, and so it was decided to establish the Toll Roads, or Turnpikes, and General Wade was appointed chief engineer. A saying of the time ran 'Had you seen this road before it was made, you would lift your hands and bless General Wade!' The Roads were divided into districts, with Turnpike Trustees respon-

Early Days on the Open Road

Sturminster Newton District Council workers building a new road in Dorset, early 1920s.

Dorset road menders with their steam roller.

sible for collecting money from travellers at toll gates, where a toll keeper lived in a small cottage and manned the gate. The tolls were very complicated, and much haggling went on between travellers and gatekeepers. Farmers driving stock of different kinds to market could be especially difficult to sort out!

Although the gates have long gone, many of the small gatekeeper's cottages survive along our roads today. The problem of the time was that once the gatekeeper had been paid out of the tolls collected, and costs of administration of the trustees had been met, there was seldom any money left over to pay for the actual repair of the roads.

By the time that motor vehicles appeared, the roads were in a pretty awful state, and there was growing debate concerning the best materials to be used, and the best way of paying for improvements.

Turning aside from the main roads, what was to happen to the network of minor roads that connected village to village? Responsibility was at first placed upon the parishes, who were required to employ roadman to do the necessary work. It has to be said that this was regarded as rather a dead end type of job, one step down from a farm labourer, and the road mender could be seen wandering along a quiet by-way, armed with barrow, pick and shovel, and occasionally giving the road a wallop with his large hammer.

Later, the Rural District Councils were given responsibility, and then that was transferred to the County Councils in 1924. If a new road was being built, much of the work would have been done by hand in 1900, with stone being quarried locally, if available, and then hauled to the site of the road in horse drawn putts. The stone would then be broken up and levelled by hand, and finally rolled by the one piece of machinery available, the Steam Roller.

The Steam Roller was the natural offspring of the Traction Engine, and certain famous companies made both machines. Aveling and Porter developed the first steam roller as early as 1865. It could take a couple of hours to raise steam in the morning, and each engine had its individual idiosyncrasies. The earlier rollers offered no protection to the driver, and it could be a very chilly job despite the proximity of the firebox and boiler.

The steam roller also had a pretty insatiable appetite for coal, and in particular, water. I remember watching one drinking water out of a small stream, using a large diameter hose with a filter on it, and

When Motoring Was Fun

the water pump driven by the engine. It almost sucked up the entire flow of water in the stream for a space of time. In areas where there was not abundant water, the rollers would tow their own water cart, built like a large cylindrical tank on two wheels, and this could be filled up using the engines pump when opportunity presented itself.

Some of the steam rollers were owned by the Council, but there were also private contractors who hired out their own teams of road menders, together with a steam roller. A special caravan was sometimes supplied, which was also towed along the roads by the steam roller. This not only provided sleeping accommodation of a pretty basic nature, but also became a small living quarters by day where a bit of cooking and tea brewing could be done, and the team could retire for a quiet smoke and spin a yarn or two when the foreman wasn't

The speed at which the steam roller moved dictated the whole pace of the operation, which took on a pleasantly leisurely quality, especially in beautiful and remote rural areas. If you were delighting in the passing countryside, and driving your car along a lane, and encountered the road men at work, you switched your engine off and settled down for a long wait. It was a good idea to carry a book in the car, otherwise you found yourself studying out of date copies of the AA yearbook! In

narrow Devon lanes it was often very difficult to find a passing place for something as large as a steam roller, and if the roller was towing its caravan and water trailer there was only one way it could proceed, and that was forwards!

Our picture below again gives a very good idea of the typical gang of road menders in the 1930s. All wear hats of some sort, to avoid excessive exposure to sun, rain or wind. Three appear to be wearing waistcoats, and only one wears true overalls. The foreman wears a jacket and tie, as the marks of his authority and position. The steam roller driver wears overalls, and seems to have a jacket of some sort over the top.

Also of interest are the implements which each man is holding, to show his particular expertise as a member of the team. We have four large brushes, and two long-tined forks, of a type specially used for this work. I am surprised there do not seem to be any large shovels in evidence.

The steam roller is again an earlier model, with no roof to keep the rain off the driver. The large rear wheels not only drove the roller, but greatly increased the surface area that it rolled.

Taking pride in their work: the Council road mending gang working near St Ervan, Cornwall, in the 1930s.

98

Early Days on the Open Road

A steam Roller working near Seaton in 1930, with attendant horse drawn putt.

Tar spraying from a lorry before re-gritting the road in Seaton about 1935.

As the years of the twentieth century rolled by, the construction of the roads became much more complicated. In 1873 the oldest concrete road was laid, and concrete was hailed by some as the best and most logical road building material. However, it did have its problems, one of which was that it proved very noisy when used by a large volume of traffic.

Incidentally, I did hear a suggestion that the steam roller driver, if away from home for a long period doing a job, might persuade his wife to take up residence in the caravan and enjoy the traveller's life, while being most useful when it came to having his meals cooked for him. This idea may have given rise to the cartoon in *Punch* which shows the wife laying out her washing in the road, and directing her husband to do her ironing by driving his steam roller over it.

This might just have worked on a concrete road that was dry and hard, but any suggestion of tar would have spoilt the week's wash entirely.

Surface dressing of the roads with tar did not start until about 1930. Heated liquid tar was forced through a spray using a hand pump that required two men to operate it. The liquid tar was transported in a specially designed horse putt, with a barrel for the tar, and a coal fire beneath it to keep it liquid and at a sprayable temperature. The putt was built with quick release shafts, so that the horses could be quickly removed from danger should the hot tar actually catch fire, something which happened from time to time. The whole gang, horses included, must have been kept on their toes! What a nightmare for Health and Safety.

Once the liquid tar had been sprayed onto the road, gravel from another local quarry, already waiting in the delivery carts, was scattered on to the road surface by hand, and then the steam roller did its work and produced a smooth finish.

Five years later the council had invested in a small tar spraying lorry which did the job more quickly, and one hopes with a much greater degree of safety. I imagine the horses at least breathed a sigh of relief at finding themselves redundant from that particular job.

As a footnote, it is interesting to learn that the average wage for men working on the roads during the 1930s was about £1.12s.0d a week. They got an extra shilling a week towards the cost of a bicycle on which to cycle to work. For some it was probably quite a long journey, depending where their gang was working.

The photograph on the page following is interesting, firstly because we have two steam rollers, and we know that this was the first time the Lowestoft to Norwich road was treated with tarmacadam. This was therefore quite a major operation. Second, we have one of the steam roller drivers sitting on top of his engine's chimney. One assumes that the fire was out, or very low, otherwise his act of bravado could have seriously damaged his prospects! It must have been quite a difficult feat to get up there, and balance on the top. Such was the great power of the camera!

The gang seem to have been joined by several onlookers from the village, which reminds us that such exciting activities could always be relied on to draw a crowd, even without someone sitting atop his chimney! The foreman of the gang does not seem to be obviously present, which may explain why time off was being taken with much enthusiasm.

Mending the roads was on the whole quite a simple task, though as the years progressed more complicated machines like Paver-Finishers appeared to do the work, and more and more men stood around watching them.

The main challenge in this country was the fact that our roads, developed as we have seen over many centuries, were simply not suited to the arrival of the motor car, much less the increasing

When Motoring Was Fun

The road mending gang outside the Hellington Bell, Bergh Apton, Suffolk, around 1911.

large commercial vehicle. This meant the frequent necessity for road widening, straightening out sharp corners, rebuilding old bridges and so on.

Actually bridges could be a little deceptive, as the experience of Totnes, situated on the River Dart in South Devon, reminds us.

Since medieval times, Totnes has been the lowest bridging point on the Dart, and the road was carried over the river by a graceful and surprisingly wide stone bridge. Up to 1944 this had served the townspeople and passing travellers exceedingly well, though the main street up through the town is narrow, and squeezes through the East Gate.

When the decision was taken that the invasion of Europe in 1944 should concentrate on Normandy, Totnes was discovered to be the gateway to many of the important ports where invasion craft would be assembled, with men and equipment. Our American allies inspected the old stone bridge over the Dart, and to use a modern expression pronounced it 'not fit for purpose.'!

There followed a conference, at which the Americans declared that there was really no problem at all, as they could easily build a new, modern, concrete bridge a bit further up river, and avoid the town completely. They also implied that such a small river as the Dart would just be regarded as a mere drainage ditch back home. The locals watched with interest as the work was begun.

An island of concrete was constructed in the centre of the softly flowing river, and a supporting

pillar erected on it. Then from the opposite banks pre-stressed and reinforced concrete roadways were constructed to meet in the middle. The whole bridge looked very serviceable, and its builders were very pleased with their work. You might even discern a slight 'we told you so' attitude.

In Devon it rains pretty much when it feels like it, all through the year, and that year March and April were especially wet, particularly up on Dartmoor. Much rainwater sloshed down into the East and West Dart, and a rapidly increasing flow of brown flood water surged down the river. When it reached Totnes, it found a novelty partially blocking its path, so it gave the centre pillar of the American's bridge a playful twist, which neatly dropped the whole structure in the river, to be washed further downstream. Fortunately it did not damage the piers of the old medieval bridge.

There was no time for further demonstrations of trans-Atlantic engineering superiority, and all the invasion traffic, by day and night, crossed the Dart using the medieval bridge, and arrived safely on schedule. The old bridge is doing duty to this day, but you now have to look very hard in the right place to detect that once there was another concrete bridge located further upstream on this beautiful and sometimes powerful river!

The road planners of the post-war period faced a challenge in the towns and cities that could not be ignored, as it daily grew worse. Broadly speaking there were three options.

The final design of steamroller, a 1921 Ruston and Hornsby engine, as restored in 1967.

The first involved doing what one could with the existing streets, by setting up a number of one way circuits, traffic lights, and also severely restricting parking. The one way streets could result in unwary drivers, unfamiliar with the town in question, entering a kind of maze from which they began to wonder whether they would ever escape. The ultimate nightmare was to imagine yourself driving down a one-way street, only to find round the corner that it was in fact a cul-de-sac. The only option left to you was to abandon your beloved car and start walking.

Such schemes proved very unpopular with the residents for two reasons. First, they were unable to drive from point A to point B along the route that they had always taken. With the new arrangement they had to drive half way round the town. Second, they were always in the habit of drawing up outside the ironmongers or the grocers, parking close to the door, and being able to load heavy packages into the car. Suddenly there were lines in the road forbidding parking, and being very law abiding, and having no hazard lights to leave flashing as a signal that parking restrictions did not apply to them, they would have to find a car park some distance from the shop, and struggle heavily laden along the pavement.

The second solution can be seen clearly in the pictures of New Street, Honiton, below. The 'Black Lion' pub has been demolished to make the street wide enough for two vehicles, and to provide a small open space and pavement, which solves the problem nicely, though it changes the whole look of the area for the benefit of the multiplying motor car. In fact the Hillman Minx in the lower picture has an almost smug look on its face! Often, it was simply not an option to pull old and valued buildings down to create the necessary space.

The third solution also involved a compromise, and that was the building of a bypass. At a stroke, this would usually solve the problem of congestion in the town.

Totnes, which as indicated above had a very narrow High Street, with a steep hill involved, not to

A drastic piece of road widening in Honiton in the early 1960s.

When Motoring Was Fun

The Plains at Totnes in 1936s. Though attractive enough, this area of the town, and the single bridge crossing the River Dart, posed a huge problem for traffic attempting to get through the town

mention the East Gate, desperately needed a solution. The final straw was when the Circus came to town, and paraded down the High Street. All went well until the elephant van jammed under the arch of the East Gate.

At once pandemonium broke loose, the procession stopped, and keepers ran to the van and gingerly led its two occupants out safely. The van promptly tried to rise several inches on its springs, being no longer weighed down with elephants, and became even more firmly stuck. Eventually they realised that the only way of getting the van through was to re-insert the elephants plus another one for luck, and then reduce the pressure in the tyres to further lower the trapped van. This was successful, and once the tyres had been inflated again the band could strike up and the procession continue on its way down to the Plains and the site for the Big Top.

Constructing one of the great arterial roads near London in the 1930s.

The problems with bypass construction were the acquisition of the necessary land, some of which might already have dwellings on it, and the fact that the traders in the town concerned would inevitably lose much of their 'passing trade.' This would especially hit garages and hotels and other businesses offering refreshment to weary travellers. However, the lack of through traffic meant that locals could once again park outside their favourite shops.

Out in the open countryside roads could be more easily widened or built because the land necessary was more readily available. However, the land was often good agricultural land, and a new road might go straight through a farm, creating many problems for the farmer. Then there were areas of natural beauty, sites of Special Scientific Interest, and colonies of highly excited toads wanting to cross the road to get to their traditional mating pond.

Into this cauldron of gently simmering problems was catapulted the environmental campaigner, ready to climb trees, burrow underground, and affix themselves to anything that would constitute a permanent obstacle to the progress of a new road.

The machines available for the construction of the new trunk roads, and ultimately the motorways were vast, and could only be afforded by huge companies in the field of building and earth moving. As a result the cost of the work escalated at an alarming rate, until today I have seen the figure of £1000 an INCH quoted!

Early Days on the Open Road

Railwaymen remind holiday motorists stuck on the notorious Exeter bypass in the 1960s that it would be quicker by rail, and you could take your car too!

In a later chapter we shall look at the problems of congestion which the multiplying motor cars produced.

One of the most famous bypasses was that around the east and south of Exeter. In the later 1950s, after the debacle of the Suez crisis had passed, and petrol was no longer rationed, a rapidly increasing holiday traffic converged on the West country. Many holiday areas like Torquay, Dartmouth, Salcombe, Looe and Falmouth expanded rapidly, catering for dinghy sailors in particular, while the lovely beaches of the North Cornish coast attracted more surf bathers.

Caravanning and camping became ever more popular, and for many holiday makers Saturday was the changeover day, when they all took to the road, either going on holiday or returning.

The majority of this Westcountry traffic had to negotiate the Exeter bypass, and it was the local opinion that many holidaymakers, going in both directions, spent most of the day within sight of the towers of Exeter Cathedral. Frustrated people would get out their picnic tables and be photographed having their mid-day meal at the roadside. It was a very accurate prophecy of what was to come, when even more cars poured out on to busy roads.

Chapter 13

THE GARAGE IN TOWN AND COUNTRY

Wardill's cycle shop and garage, Pound Street, Carshalton, in about 1912.

In considering the role of the garage, it is perhaps a help to specify three different varieties, all fairly essential to the motorist.

First came the motorist's own local base, his garage at home. He might himself live in a large cold house, but as we have already indicated his garage must be warm, dry and snug. It should have a pit, covered over with wooden planks of at least two inches thickness, so that the motorist can easily remove them, and descend underneath his precious car, there to inspect all its undercarriage, and incidentally do his lumbago no good at all in the process!

Beside the spot where his car rests, he should have a spacious workbench, which should be uncluttered, but seldom is. Beside that should be a large tool cupboard, equipped with every type of spanner and wrench, and a good strong heavy hammer for 'last resort' tactics! A loft above is useful for storing the larger spare parts like exhaust systems and mudguards.

At home in Devon we had a large and splendid three car garage, which the swallows colonised each year for nesting purposes. My father, a great bird lover, rigged up a sort of horizontal screen to catch all the droppings before they fell on the car below.

Meanwhile the advertisements of the day offered a wide variety of essentials for the enthusiastic motorist, as standard equipment for his garage. He must have an accumulator charger, and a supply of electricity. He will need vulcanisers for his tyres, and valve grinders. Motor stethoscopes are the only way of locating those elusive 'knocks' and patent lubricators just might cure them. Petrol must not be kept in the garage, it was always supplied in those distinctive metal cans, and should be put in a building some distance away. In fact many motorists dug a hole in the garden and buried their reserve supply. At the time of the Suez crisis my father erected a new and empty beehive, and put his emergency reserve petrol into it. He figured no one would want to investigate too closely!

104

A wonderful photograph of cars outside Beaminster garage in Dorset about 1920.

An assortment of spare tyres, inner tubes, wire and tape could be hung on the walls to give a festive appearance, together with one or two old advertisements for sparking plugs and the like.

Second comes the motorists own local garage. A very good example of what it might be like is shown in the photograph at the start of this chapter, taken about 1912 in Carshalton. Here it is obvious that Mr. Wardill is in the process of adding cars to his cycle workshop. The sign on the right shows that he is an agent for Pratts Motor Spirit, and in fact his garage business grew apace from this time onwards. In other instances it was the local Blacksmith who branched out and developed his repertoire, but not always. Mr Atwill, the blacksmith in my home village in Devon, remained dedicated to the horse alone to the end of his days.

We were very lucky with both our local garages as already recorded. Douglas Harris was a fine mechanic, and I vividly remember that he let me help him change the engine in my 1954 Hillman Husky, which not only added an extra pair of sometimes helpful hands, but also taught me a great deal about the inner workings of my car.

Garages could be tucked away in strange places. The lovely photograph above of Beaminster Garage

taken in about 1920 indicates that you had to cross a bridge over the stream beside the road to enter the premises.

The signpost, a lovely touch, advertises Pratts Perfection Spirit, Shell, Vacuum Oils and Avon Tyres, while the garage offers Repairs, Overhauling, Vulcanising and Accessories. Arthur Hann and Albert Hann, relatives of Cecil Hann, the manager, are the drivers of the two cars. Both cars are worthy of note. The one on the left is probably a 6 cylinder Lanchester Sporting 60, and the one on the right is an American 1913 R.C. Hupp 22hp Tourer, with Dorset trade plates, presumably imported for a client.

In my own case I was wandering through the mid-Welsh town of Builth Wells when I noticed an alley way with an old sign up on the wall saying 'Builth Motor Company.' Rather intrigued I went in and looked round the corner. It turned out to be the back premises of the garage which fronted onto the High Street, and there sitting amongst the stinging nettles, looking a little forlorn was Victoria, a black 1954 Riley RME 1½ litre saloon. That was the moment which re-kindled my interest in older cars, and has led to the restoration of six of them, and the writing of some books!

In most cases, if the motorist was wise, he would cultivate a good relationship with his local garage, and try to be as loyal as possible, for he never knew from one day to the next when he might need their

Hand operated petrol pumps at Manaton Garage on Dartmoor about 1939.

Filling up a car at Bridestowe in Devon with hand operated pump in the mid 1930s.

services, and sometimes an emergency would require help pretty urgently.

Obtaining a supply of petrol would be part of that loyalty. In a town one would visit the garage and be presented with a bewildering array of pumps offering different brands. There would be Cleveland and Total, Esso and Shell, BP and Derv, to name a few. Then there was my fathers favourite tipple, National Benzole Mixture. He was quite sure there must be a drop of whisky in it which was good for the car. Failing that he would substitute a few drops of Redex, which I still use myself, but only in the car I hasten to add, to improve performance.

Once you had made your choice, you put four gallons into the tank, parted with five shillings, received a copper or two change , and drove on your way duly refreshed.

But suppose you lived in the depths of the country? You would drive down to the local Blacksmith, and wait patiently while he finished off shoeing a horse. He would then emerge, wiping his hands on his sacking apron, and you would ask for four

A very smart parade at Manor Garage, Brundall in Norfolk, in 1936.

Early Days on the Open Road

Another garage parade at Widecombe-in-the-Moor, Devon in about 1952.

gallons. There was no choice, as there was only one pump! He would remove your filler cap, and pocket it, and place the tap on the end of the pump hose in the filler, turned off. He would then wind the handle on the front of the pump, and you would both watch as the level of petrol rose in the sort of goldfish bowl on top of the pump. When you were both happy it had come to rest on the line, Mr Smith would open the tap, and one gallon of petrol would shoot down into your tank, propelled by gravity. The operation would be repeated three more times, you would help Mr Smith discover where he had put your filler cap, and having parted with your five shillings you would go confidently on your way. There were many villages in the 1920s and 30s which still had no electricity, so this was the only possible type of petrol pump. Some even survived into the 1940s and very early 50s.

In the picture of Brundall on the previous page we see two typical cars of the 1930s arranged for the display. On the left is the ubiquitous Morris 8 from the mid 1930s, of which we had two examples in the family after the war, one of them mine. The other car is a much grander Armstrong Siddeley saloon, of rather earlier vintage. The bins between the pumps would contain engine and lubricating oils like Castrol. In this picture the petrol pumps are electrically operated, and BP, National Benzole Mixture and Shell are the choice offered. Are the people in the picture two garage staff and two motorists? It does look like it. It is certainly a very typical garage scene from the 1930s.

As the years passed, the local garage developed. Electric power was a great boon, not only with petrol pumps but with lighting too. Inspection lamps made it much easier to investigate the underside of a car in trouble.

The local garage took to keeping an increasing stock of the most commonly used spare parts for cars, and especially those cars most popular in the district. This led by stages to stocking items which local motorists could buy, like tins of engine oil and sparking plugs. As time went by it became sensible to stock batteries and spares and accessories for bicycles, as well as some hardware items, but in rural communities where there could often be a General Store in the village, the garage would be careful to avoid food items and other things which could compete. Friendship and community spirit were more important than making as much money as possible.

I could not resist putting in the picture opposite because of the team of six garage staff on parade. Beard's Garage in Widecombe was a family run business, and in the centre of the group are Wilfred Beard (with the cap on), and Gwen Beard beside him. It appears that Wilfred has just given the order 'stand at ease' to the company!

The petrol pumps at this garage are interesting, because they appear to be one up to date electric pump, the Esso one on the left, and one older type hand operated pump on the right. On the left another member of staff wears a cap and uniform, and may be the driver of the Austin 16 saloon of late 1940s vintage, which I suspect the garage used as a taxi, and which would have been most useful for local people.

The third class of garage was the one you happened upon when on a journey. The most important factor for such garages was their position. They needed to be on a main road, but preferably at the edge of a town or village, where a speed limit meant that passing traffic was slowed down.

Such garages concentrated a lot on their appearance, as this was what would attract a passing motorist, much as a flower seeks to attract a passing bee. In fact a few well placed flower beds, carefully tended, drawing attention to welcoming signs advertising the facilities offered by the garage were often to be seen.

Lisle's Garage, situated on the outskirts of Woolmer Green in Hertfordshire, on the Great North Road is a classic example. By the 1950s it had an eye catching canopy over the Esso petrol pumps, which would attract any motorist especially on a rainy day, and as soon as a car drew up the pump attendant would emerge from his little office, and attend to the needs of the motorist, offering oil, air and water as required as well as the petrol, and even washing the windscreen, a very desirable service before the coming of the windscreen washer.

Lisle's Garage as it had developed by the 1950s.

Lisle's Garage in Woolmer Green in the 1920s.

Park Langley Garage, Beckenham, in 1929.

The cars shown in the top photograph are a Ford V8 Pilot on the left, and a 1.5 litre Jaguar on the right, both looking very smart indeed. On one occasion a lorry had difficulty manoeuvring between the pumps, and pushed the little attendants hut off its concrete base. The garage owner was quite equal to the challenge. He got another lorry, drove it round the back, and pushed the hut back into position!

The story of Lisle's garage is fairly typical, but the Park Langley Garage at Beckenham is surely worthy of special note, as the two pictures (right) show. The garage, which includes covered forecourt and pumps, is in an Oriental style of architecture, and the staff wore caps, ties, and plum coloured livery. The petrol offered was BP or Pratts, and the petrol pumps must be some of the most elaborate hand

Park Langley Garage petrol pumps in use.

operated pumps in the country. It is appropriate that the car being attended to is a very smart saloon, possibly an American model, but it is difficult to be certain from the backside!

The need for such garages in the early days was a pressing one, as a couple of travellers tales well illustrate.

For two years after he acquired his first car, a De Dion, Kenneth Murchison kept a 'Motoring Diary.' This is his account of a trip in North Wales in 1903.

Left Menai at 9.a.m. Called at Bangor for a new tyre. Could not get one. Ran over a sheep. At Bethesda changed gears so rapidly that I broke the connecting rod of the steering gear. Being at the top of a long hill there was nothing for it but to go down the hill backwards in the hope of getting down the hill alive and finding a blacksmith. This was done; slate quarry workers on strike and much interested in car.

After wait of 2½ hours blacksmith finished his job, but the product of his labour was 1/16 of an inch too small. Waited another 2 ½ hours, this time a successful result. Going round a sharp corner nearly ran into a large lake...

Dr Tracey arrived in Willand, Devon, with his wife Emily in 1894, and soon established a very successful practice. In 1907, with his wife's financial backing, he became the first man to own a car in the district, a 10/12hp Peugeot. He also kept a motoring diary, and some of the entries are as follows:

19th Sept. 1907. Car arrives. Willand to Tiverton Junction and back.
8th October. Ran over and damaged S.H.Thomas's dog. Its own fault entirely owing to almost complete deafness.

12th October. Rotten French tyre burst through puncture in Cullompton. Stuck on two awful hills. Got her up empty.
25th October. Met a herd of cows 3 miles the other side of Totnes. Bent axle, steering rod, lamp brackets. Damaged lamps, much of this because of striking hedge after striking 2 or 3 cows.
6th November. Exeter and back. Took Alice and Miss Lewis. A very pleasant ride. Foot brake loose again. In consequence hit a post in our yard and knocked it up. Chick mended it.

He was apparently a very good and much loved doctor, but one cannot help feeling that local animals must have fled when they saw his car coming!

In the picture below of Pimperne Garage we are reminded that in the early days in rural areas many garages advertised themselves as Motor and Agricultural Engineers. No tractors in sight here, but an impressive line up of two Standard Vanguards, a Morris, an Austin Devon Pickup and an older Morris 12. The scene pictured picture is dated about 1954, and later in 1990 the Garage became one owned by Nigel Mansell, the Formula One World Champion, before becoming Westover Sports Cars.

The outside of the garage might change with the times, but sometimes the inside had a sort of timeless quality. Here we see the two aspects of the garages work, the sales of vehicles, which we have already encountered, and the repairing of customers cars. Mechanics were true craftsmen in the early days, able to diagnose the problem of the car, and to put it right. They could cope with any make of car that appeared, though they might look a

Pimperne Garage with selection of cars. 1954.

When Motoring Was Fun

little bewildered when confronted with some huge and complicated American beast!

I do remember a mechanic in Wells, to whom I turned in dire need when the water pump went on my almost new rear-engined Hillman Imp, assuring me that he knew exactly what to do, and then looking decidedly baffled when he lifted the bonnet in front!

When we went on holiday in 1983, we were partly getting ideas for my eldest son's first car, and couldn't help exploring one of the most untidy and exciting garages I have ever been into, in Pembroke. The owner was conducting a very lengthy conversation on the phone, so we explored the back of the garage, and I suddenly realised that the huge heap of garage jumble in the corner had the general shape of a car about it. We moved one or two pieces, and sure enough revealed a small part of a 1930s Austin radiator.

Quite excited, we tackled Mr Jones when he surfaced, but though genial he would not contemplate any sort of a deal.

'The thing is, boyo,' he said, 'I shall be restoring that lovely car in a little while myself, so I couldn't be selling it to you, now could I?'

We had to leave it at that, but I did notice that the newspapers with which it was covered were of 1961 date!

Over the next twenty years we visited Pembroke on a fairly regular basis, it being a favourite holiday spot, and always called in on Mr Jones to buy petrol. Each time we had a look in the corner of the garage, and the old Austin was still there, though rather more obscured by covering layers of junk on each occasion.

Trevetts Garage interior, in Harbour Road, Seaton about 1937, with staff on parade.

Sadly, on our last visit two years ago the garage had closed, and obviously gone out of business. The windows had been painted over, so there was no way of seeing whether the familiar heap was still present in the far left hand corner!

Garages today are very different places, because they have to cope with a very different kind of car. However, I do know of one or two where the inside is much as it always has been, and you can still find a real mechanic, which is essential if you run a pre-war car on a regular basis.

In the photograph of the interior of Elliott's garage in Bideford we see a potential customer sitting in a nice tourer, with a dickey seat which suggests it may be a Morris Cowley. One of the three men is a member of the garage staff, but the other two, wearing identical hats, might be twin brothers. Neither seems inclined to climb into the driving seat. Number plates suggest that both cars in view are second hand models.

Elliott's Garage in Bideford, showing interior in about 1934.

Chapter 14

DOWN ON THE FARM

The 1930s and the age of the horse on farms is fast giving way to steam tractor power.

In 1900 there were two sources of motive power in the countryside. The heavy horse had held sway for many centuries, and was still powerful, versatile, and loved by all countrymen who paused to watch them at work. They could plough and harrow, rake and reap, pull loads to the top of a stack using a derrick, and pull every kind of cart, with two or four wheels. Only when it came to jobs like threshing were they caught lacking.

Mounting the challenge to the horse was the newly developed traction engine, now being refined and made more powerful. Two engines and a rig could plough a field at a remarkable speed, and the engine was ideal for powering the new threshing machines and elevators. A threshing team with an engine could go from farm to farm and speed up the process greatly, as well as providing much entertainment to local people, especially small boys!

However, the tractions engines did not like steep hills or sloping fields, as they had quite a high centre of gravity, so while the east of England suited

them well, there were large areas of the country which did not, and where the horse continued to reign supreme.

The tractor was fairly slow to develop in Britain due to two factors; the nature of the land, and the competition. We do not have the vast fields of North America or Australia. However, as we have seen with other vehicles, the First World War meant that development was greatly speeded up, and especially concerning vehicles to tackle challenging cross country conditions.

Such tractors could either be provided with large rear wheels, or with caterpillar tracks, like the new tanks.

In 1930 the Ford Motor Company started to produce their new Fordson tractor at their plant at Cork, in Ireland, and a few years later the operation was transferred to Dagenham in Essex. This tractor had the standard design which was to be found for the next forty years or more, with radiator at the front, and starting handle below. The engine was

When Motoring Was Fun

The excellent cab fitted to Herbert Hart's tractor at Haughley Green in about 1939.

mounted behind the front wheels, and then the driver sat on a seat between the large rear wheels which carried the drive. The gearbox was between the driver's legs, and from his position he had an excellent view reversing, or picking up trailers and other implements. The engine was very reliable, and the tractor strong, and with a good performance across rough ground, especially when fitted with spiked wheels.

Farmers have always been a resourceful type of person, and in certain areas where the wind whistles strong and cold it could get very chilly indeed driving your tractor for hours at a time, even if fortified with a thermos of tea and a hip flask of something stronger!

Suffolk is one of those places where 'lazy winds' blow from the north and east, especially at cultivating time, and so Herbert Hart, who worked on Mrs Lingley's farm at Old Hall, Haughley Green, decided that something needed to be done. The result, skilfully built onto the back of the standard Fordson Tractor, looks like part of the body of a small caravan. I imagine the access door was round the back, but it is certainly a wonderful creation, and would have given excellent visibility as well as being remarkably snug. No wonder Herbert has a very satisfied smile on his face. He must have been the envy of every other tractor driver in the district. This tractor, in the picture below, is fitted with the spiked rear wheels which would have been very necessary on heavy Suffolk clay. The picture also shows the layout of the tractor very well, with air intake to the carburettor, and exhaust pipe.

When the Fordson tractor was first introduced, it was painted in a striking orange, and was visible from afar, which was probably intentional. But by the hot summer of 1940, times had changed, as the following conversation recorded at an aerodrome in Northern France reveals.

'Ach, mein Kapitaine, I haf just achieved a great victory!'

'Vot is it you haf done, mein Hanz?'

'Mein Kapitaine, I have disrupted and destroyed the whole agriculture of the accursed English.'

'Zat is brilliant. How vas it done?'

'I have shot up a bright orange tractor. The driver has run for ze life. I am deserving of the Iron Cross, nein?'

In fact, the Luftwaffe pilots had discovered that the bright orange tractors were an easier and more comfortable target than a Spitfire, and defended with nothing but an old shotgun, if that. Every farmer in southern England rushed to his store shed and dug out that old can of green or brown paint, and executed a camouflage job on his tractor that was worthy of any branch of the Armed Forces. So the precious tractors lay low throughout the war, undetected from above, and then after the war the new ones were painted a tasteful blue, and continued their excellent work down on the farm.

As early as 1931 Harry Ferguson came up with a brilliant idea. He devised a three-point attachment system for implements on the back of a standard

Early Days on the Open Road

Harold Wearne, of Sennen, Cornwall, on his Ferguson TE-20 cutting a field of white oats in the late 1940s.

type tractor. Ferguson teamed up with David Brown, who was already making tractors, and the first product was the 'Black Tractor' in 1933. The Ferguson-Brown partnership foundered, and in 1938 Ferguson gave a remarkable display of his tractors abilities to Henry Ford. In June 1939 the first Ford-Ferguson tractor was produced, and in the first year ten thousand were sold. In 1946 Ford and Ferguson split, rather unhappily, and Harry Ferguson set up his own plant to produce his tractors. The first model was the TE-20, known to everyone as the 'grey Fergie' and produced in 1947. It is pictured above.

This tractor, light in weight yet powerful, small and versatile, became a great favourite throughout the countryside. Harry Ferguson used the engine from the Standard Vanguard car to power his tractor, and extended the range of implements that would fit onto it.

Quite a lot of my early learning to drive was done on a grey Fergie, and it was a delight to handle. Later, when in the army, I was required to do tests on gun and generator deployment around an airfield. The plan was that the guns and generators would be dropped by parachute, together with a grey Fergie tractor, which would be used to tow the equipment into position.

We did our tests on a disused airfield, in icy snow covered conditions. The tractor was quite capable of towing the heavy equipment over the relatively flat ground, and could build up to a respectable speed while doing so. The problem came when you wanted to stop. There were no brakes on the equipment, and I have vivid memories of sitting on the tractor and being pushed for many yards along the runway with no apparent decrease in speed at all, in spite of having all the tractor brakes on and using the engine for braking as well. It was all a bit scary, and I don't think the idea was taken any further after my report!

The Hutchings family of Sennen riding their grey Fergie in the 1950s.

A mixed group of tractors, including David Brown, Grey Fergie and Fordson, clearing ground for a playing field at Mylor, Cornwall, in 1947.

113

When Motoring Was Fun

Land Girls driving the tractors at Castle Green Farm, Leigh, in the early 1940s.

Four Land Girls in Beaminster, Dorset, wait to be driven out to work on the farms, c.1943.

Typical rural transport of delight – Sam Cannon, farm labourer of Widecombe-in-the-Moor, Dartmoor, with dog and BSA motorbike in the 1930s.

The Second World War brought great changes down on the farm, just as the first war had done.

The attempt by Hitler to starve the British people into submission by sinking every ship coming to our islands with supplies, prompted the 'Dig for Victory' campaign, and the desperate project to maximise the productivity of our farms. Every square foot was cultivated, and farmers became expert at improvisation where necessary. Due to the many farm labourers called up into the forces, labour became a problem, and the Womens Land Army was formed.

These ladies became known as the 'Land Girls' and performed an invaluable role throughout the war, not only showing huge skills and stamina, but enlivening the countryside no end. They became expert tractor drivers in many cases, as the picture above reminds us. Here we see four of the Land Girls on typical tractors of the period, an International, two Fordsons, and another International on the right. All would have needed to be started at times on the handle, and that required strength and skill.

The Land Girls were accommodated in Hostels, and driven out to the farms where they worked in a War Agricultural Executive Committee van like the one pictured above, with its four smiling passengers.

Near Crediton, Devon, German P.O.W. 'Heinz' poses with a Fordson Major tractor.

Later on in the war period a new source of Agricultural workers presented itself, in the form of German Prisoners of War. It must have badly upset the Fuhrer to think that his ex troops were helping the British produce more food on their farms! For the P.O.W.'s life and work on the farms was much preferable to being cooped up in a camp, however relaxed the conditions were, and in many cases they made real friends with the families they were sent to help. They also discovered that the food available on the farms was very much better than anything up at the camp! In the picture above a P.O.W. poses for the camera on the newly introduced Fordson Major tractor, during probably the last year of the war.

During the war, and after it, there was a lot of machinery to keep running down on the farm, and farmer had to be resourceful mechanics with a gift for improvisation if things were to go smoothly. They also had to keep their eyes open for any vehicle that could be pressed into service.

When I did my National Service in the later 1950s, I was, as recorded, posted to Western Wales, and found time for a little rough shooting, mainly rabbits, which were welcomed by the mess steward. I was wandering round Mr Jones' farm at Penarth one summers evening, when I noticed something curious about the bramble patch where my bob tailed quarry had taken refuge.

Some probing with a handy stick revealed the familiar triangle shaped radiator, with the red RR on it! A further look round revealed that the bramble patch was concealing a complete chassis and engine, but the body had been removed. Later in the evening I saw Mr Jones, and asked him about it.

'Oh, yes, that old car now' he said thoughtfully. 'You see, my brother is an undertaker, Liverpool way, and when he has finished with a car, now, he ships them down for me to use on the farm. See here, now, I've got another one out here in the yard.'

He led me out into the farmyard, and there in a corner was a huge stately Rolls-Royce hearse, being used as a very up-market chicken house.

I asked Mr Jones if he would ever consider selling the cars, and he looked very thoughtful again and said he would have to ask ten pounds each for them. Since twenty pounds a month was about my salary as a most junior National Service officer, I had to decline, but I did mention the presence of the cars to a friend in the mess, a Regular Army Captain, and when a year or two later I went again in search of the cars they had gone.

Farmers cars were almost universally large, solid, and extremely dirty, having been used for every sort of farm occupation, and never washed in their lives! James Herriot tells the story of a memorable encounter with such a car, a large old saloon from the 1920s, which crashes into their new Rover while trying to overtake a lorry. The old car ends up in the ditch, and when James is at last able to open a door, a cloud of screaming hens hurtle out, to reveal the farmer covered in egg, but with a silly grin on his face all the same.

Farmers cars would have been frequently used to take all manner of things to market, including quite large livestock. It was always a good idea to examine the back seat carefully before sitting on it! The arrival of the Austin 18 in the 1930s provided the farmers with the ideal vehicle. It was robust and quite powerful, with large wheels for cross country work, very comfortable, and with a roomy interior which would take a middling sized cow! I remember as a boy that quite a number of local farmers had this particular car, and on market day you could see them all lined up, waiting for their owners to conclude their business and emerge from the pub.

A team of four plus dog get in the Hay harvest at North Road Farm, High Bickington, Devon, in 1950.

Combine harvester in Suffolk, on manor Farm, Elmsett, in 1936.

Children ride on the tractor at Bushey Ley, near Elmsett, in 1947, before the arrival of Health and Safety.

Meanwhile after the war the old Fordson tractor was superseded by the much improved Fordson Major tractor, pictured below. This was a larger tractor, with better ground clearance and more power. Painted blue, it became a much used resident on thousands of farms, and gained a well deserved reputation for reliability. The family group below seem very proud of their Fordson!

As we have noted, one aftermath of the Second World War was a large number of ex-American Army Jeeps, which it did not seem worth while to transport back to the USA and which were consequently sold off cheap in this country and on the continent.

Many a farmer spotted the potential of these little vehicles, with their powerful engines and four wheel drive engineering. They were snapped up, and soon inspired the Rover company to bring out the Land Rover. With this rugged vehicle farmers could drive round their farms in a degree of comfort which a tractor had never accorded them. They could also easily accommodate a small pack of dogs as well, and the farm dogs took to cross country transport with enthusiasm. Following a Land Rover along a country lane one often saw two or three dogs heads sticking out of the passenger window savouring the breeze, or leaning out of the back admiring the view!

In the 1930s other machinery appeared on British farms, and none was more impressive to us as youngsters than the Combine Harvester. Getting in the harvest in good condition had always been a great challenge for farmers, and especially in a country where summer weather could never be guaranteed, and a heavy shower of thundery rain could give stooked corn a thorough wetting.

The earlier combines had to be towed by a tractor, and in the picture above a Field Marshall Diesel, a most distinctive tractor of the 1930s, is doing duty. Two other remarkable features of this machine are the off set cutter, a contrast with today's machines, and the unusual corn hopper. The combine is seen in 1936, unloading into the back of a lorry of the period. Three members of the Cooper family, John, Harold and Percy are managing the whole harvesting operation, a significant contrast to the process ten years before.

This Case Combine Harvester was restored by the Cooper Family and made it's appearance again at Manor Farm, Elmsett, in the 1990s.

When the tractor towed machines gave way to the self-propelled Combine, the farmer could sit up above his field as lord of all he surveyed, and drive great swathes through the standing corn. The whole procedure of corn harvesting became much easier, except on those rather too frequent occasions when the harvesting transport of delight suffered a breakdown. It was very frustrating for an arable farmer to be waiting for days for a vital spare part for his machine, and at the same time watching the storm clouds gathering ominously on the horizon!

The coming of this great machine, and the straw bailers that soon followed it, brought a revolution to the countryside, and one of great benefit to the farmers, however much those with a strong nostalgic streak might bemoan the passing of the old steam driven threshing team.

Before the Combine harvester, a Fordson Tractor and binder cuts the corn at Court Place farm, Withycombe in the 1930s.

Cousin Edward in later middle age decided that he had never really wanted to devote his life to the Cooperage business in Tottenham High Road, so he sold off the eight acres for an amazing sum of money, and migrated down to Devonshire to be a farmer, buying two adjacent farms for the purpose. Edward was determined to be a 'hands on' farmer, and in fact nothing delighted him more than driving tractors. His fascination for new and complicated machinery made him the perfect prey for the Farm Equipment salesman, and before long there were a dozen tractors on one farm alone, all pretty well brand new.

The reason was that no-one had explained to Edward that you could disconnect one implement from a tractor, and fit another. Thus when we visited the farm, we found the dozen tractors scattered about, each apparently abandoned when in the middle of a job. There was even a new digger sitting in the middle of a patch of marshy ground at the far side of the lawn, which looked as though it would need some skilful extraction.

While we were with my brother, Cousin Edward phoned to say he had just purchased the latest hydraulic muck loader, complete with tractor, and where was there some muck he could practice on? We met him beside a muck heap at the corner of a field, and he went into action at once.

On his first run at the heap, he aimed the prongs too low, and they dug into the ground, with the result that the tractor very nearly somersaulted over the heap, driver and all. Edward then over corrected, and on the second attempt just got a small armful of muck off the top of the heap. Finally, after some time, the manure spreader, christened by my brother the 'Cow dung flinger,' had a reasonable load, and after some debate it was decided where to spread it.

My brother warned us to stand well clear, and then battened down his tractor cab as best he could. When the machine was activated, the whole scene was hidden by a great cloud of flying dung, which went in every direction. The first time my brother used the machine he did not know what to expect, and left the rear of the cab open. He said he was coated from hair to seat in a layer about two inches thick!

Not every transport of delight can produce such a remarkable spectacle, or smell so rich and rural, but alas down on the farm most transport comes to its appointed end sooner or later. Below we see a sort of tractor graveyard, mainly for Grey Fergies, by the look of it, but in my experience most vehicles are just left where they die, like the Rolls-Royce in the bramble patch, and gently disintegrate over the passing years.

Chapter 15

LUGGAGE AND OTHER CARGO

A variety of vehicles outside the Royal Clarence Hotel, Bridgwater, about the year 1910.

In the days when the poorer members of the population travelled in a gig or pony trap, or on the stage coach for longer distances, it appears they had to make do with a minimum of luggage, because there was very little space to put it. For the rich, of course, it was a different matter, and the titled persons in Georgette Heyer's ever accurate stories always had a second coach following loaded with the necessary baggage.

This state of affairs seems to have been carried over into the age of the motor car. The first cars, it must be admitted, had very little space for anything, including passengers. However, as the car developed about 1910, possibilities for the carriage of extras were seriously explored. As noted, running boards could accommodate spare wheels, as well as batteries and tool chests. If your car had a fabric hood, putting anything on top was asking for trouble. If it had a saloon roof, it was probably too high to reach, even if you stood on the running board, and fixing anything up there would be a big problem.

In the picture above of Bridgwater High Street and the Royal Clarence Hotel about 1910, there are some interesting details. The carter has no problem carrying cargo, for that is what his cart is designed for, though his horse does look a trifle bored with proceedings. The car behind is of great interest, for it carries an unusual cargo, and this has to go on the roof because there is nowhere else to put it. It is a mattress shaped container holding the gas on which the car engine ran. Later, in war time conditions, they were to become much more of a feature, but always up on the roof, which may have been the safest place to carry such a highly inflammable cargo!

My own first car, the Morris 8 1936 tourer, offered little possibility for putting cargo on the outside. But I quickly made a very valuable discovery. The base of the back seat simply lifted out, being contained by a metal lip about an inch deep. You could then tilt the back of the seat forward, and lift it clear, as it just had two positioning pins which

Early Days on the Open Road

Citroen half tracks on a 2000 mile journey across the Sahara in the 1930s.

went into holes in the floor at the back. This, as I remember, provided a ledge about four feet square or more, plus the foot well for the back seat passengers. For such a small car it was an amazing amount of totally unencumbered space, and if you then put the hood down the amount of headroom was infinite! I could carry a huge variety of cargo in the back of that little car, with very easy loading over either side as desired!

Meanwhile the larger cars were tackling the luggage problem with a will. This was the period when roof racks and luggage carriers became widespread, and more and more cars were designed with boots. A number of cars still had the spare wheel carried on a bracket on the rear panel, so a boot was not possible, but other designs opted for a special compartment above the rear bumper, where the spare wheel was carried flat, behind the petrol tank. This left space above for a boot, but its carrying capacity was very limited.

It did, however, have one advantage, and that was the ability to open the boot lid, leave it open, and pile more luggage on top of it. Luckily its construction was usually robust, and it would support the weight of a school trunk. In our family school trunks were a big challenge, and were even sent by rail, Passenger Luggage in Advance, while the humans travelled by car. The trunks were too heavy to travel on the roof, and it was a great day when the first Land Rover arrived and solved all the problems at a stroke.

On one famous occasion we did try the school run in the Jowett Javelin, taking out the rear seat base, putting a school trunk in its place, and putting the base back on top. Both my brother and I travelled in turns lying flat on the seat base, just beneath the roof of the car, and both my brother and I took it in turns to be very sick as a result!

In the most opulent cars there were fitted cock-tail cabinets and hampers, but still the problem of bulky ordinary luggage persisted.

In darkest Africa and similar situations everything had to be piled into ones vehicle, leaving hopefully just enough room for the driver. My father on safari, shown earlier in this book, is a reminder of this challenge, and if you were setting out to cross the Sahara, then a huge amount of cargo had to be carried, as the picture above testifies.

A good deal of this cargo was presumably water, for humans and vehicles alike.

Two rather fascinating examples involve houses and garages. A garage for your precious car was always most important, and one company solved the problem by producing the 'Mousetrap' portable model.

This garage, seen below, worked on a hinge and 'could be lifted by a child' according to the advertisement. It seems a very suitable solution when one has a small space, and a small car as well, but it is not very clear how portable it was. Did you tow it behind the car, or did it have a window that lined

The mousetrap portable garage of the 1920s.

When Motoring Was Fun

up with the windscreen, so that you drove along with it over the top of the car? There are many possibilities, all based on the model of the snail, and indeed when the garage became portable it may well be that the vehicle could only move at a snails pace!

We have most of us seen portable homes being transported on large lorries down the road, but from across the Atlantic comes a different idea, and one which I suppose was the 1930s forerunner of the now common motor home. However, in this case one does have to truly marvel at the style of the conveyance, though one does wonder how it handled on the open road, and what it was like doing maintenance when necessary. It does look as though a good deal would have to be taken apart to change a wheel, for instance. The balcony on the back, however, is a real inspiration, and there must have been room inside for most of ones household effects!

There were certainly times when human cargo was the order of the day and they could be carried in a variety of ways. The picture below shows

A true motor home and family seen in an American town in the 1930s.

Thornes 'all purpose double-decker vehicle' and I have included it mainly because of the remarkable seating arrangement on the roof, and the apparent unconcern of the two passengers up there at their predicament. How they got up and down is a mystery, but one can imagine their speedy reaction when a low bridge hove in sight! One can also suggest, quite fairly I think, that with totally unsprung roof seats, and solid tyres, a journey of any length must have been extremely painful for a certain part of the lower anatomy!

Mr Thorne, the carrier, of Cerne Abbas, in Dorset, with his amazing vehicle, about 1913.

Early Days on the Open Road

A lorry load of happy students from Selwyn College, British Solomon Islands, in 1970.

Meanwhile in certain far flung posts of Empire the problem of moving numbers of people was easily solved by simply inviting them to stand on the back of a lorry. In the picture above a party of students prepare to set out on a journey from their college that will either be wet and muddy, or dry and dusty, and will anyway require a considerable balancing skill going round corners and through deep pot holes!

In the more rural areas of our land, like Suffolk, there is another cargo carrier which is seldom seen, but most vital none the less. This is the beaters' trailer. It is usually constructed from an ordinary two or four wheel trailer, with a canopy supported on metal hoops, and with either wooden or metal seats with or without cushions of doubtful pedigree, or else with straw bales round the sides. Access is via the back, and sometimes a step is provided. There is usually some sort of gate to confine dogs on board when under way.

As can be seen, the advantage of the straw-baled model was that at lunch time the bales could be lifted out of the trailer, and tastefully arranged on the grass so that the beaters could eat in comfort. The dogs all gathered round and usually did pretty well. In the front of the trailer would be a row of hooks, and here any game that had been shot would be hung up. By the end of a strenuous day, the inside of the trailer grew pretty fuggy, with the smell of game mingled with wet dogs and ripe beaters! The trailer would usually be towed by a tractor or Land Rover, and if it did get stuck in the mud there were plenty of people to give it a push.

A beaters' trailer, with its occupants enjoying their picnic lunch. Sussex about 1990.

The picture on the following page reminds us that there was often scope for a bit of improvisation. The grey Fergie tractor was not a load carrying vehicle, in fact a driver and a couple of passengers hanging on was about the limit, and a bit risky at that, but suppose you could lay your hands on a couple of railway trucks and a length of rope, then you really were in business!

The esparto grass, incidentally, was grown in North Africa, and was used in the making of paper, not for animal feed, so it was worth bringing ship loads over to Watchet. Loading and unloading the grass by hand must have been a pretty boring occupation, however.

When I first moved away from home in Devon to work in Suffolk, I frequently went on about the paradise I had left, and in particular the fact that because we supplied cider apples to the local factory, we could buy barrels of draught cider for sixpence a pint. At length my work colleagues had had enough of this propaganda, and they surrounded me and demanded that next time I returned to this fabled land of the cider, I should bring them each back a ten-gallon barrel.

121

When Motoring Was Fun

John Tudball of Watchet uses his grey Fergie to haul a cargo of esparto grass in the 1950s.

In due course I returned to Devon on holiday, driving the Mk 2 Land Rover, and paid a visit to the cider factory as instructed. I discovered that if I put the spare wheel on the bracket mounted on the bonnet, the well in the back would exactly accommodate six ten-gallon barrels as though designed for that exact purpose! I was a little sensitive about my liquid cargo, so covered over the barrels with an old blanket.

Once again I decided on a night journey, and so 2am found me cruising along the old North Circular Road in almost traffic free conditions. In the distance, I spotted a light, moving to and fro in a horizontal manner, and as I got closer to it, I perceived that it was attached to a large policeman, so I came to a stop. He approached my driver's window, and you couldn't have found a nicer policeman in the whole country.

'I'm so sorry to stop you, sir, but we have a small problem.'

'What is that, officer?' I asked.

'Well sir, one of our highly valued residents from Wormwood Scrubs prison just down the road has decided to have a night out, and so we have to check all the cars going past just in case he's hitched a lift.'

'Don't worry at all, Officer.' I said. 'I quite understand the situation.'

The policeman shone his torch past the back of my seat and into the rear of the Land Rover. He seemed to be overcome with embarrassment.

'I hate to ask you this sir, but could you be so kind as to show me what you have under that there blanket?'

I reached round and whipped off the blanket, and the policeman's eyes nearly popped out of his head.

'I get very thirsty when I'm driving at night' I said.

The policeman roared with laughter, and replied 'If I wasn't on duty, sir, I'd be joining you!

Today I suspect I would be subjected to a breath test, and spend the rest of the night in a police cell, but there was more of a sense of proportion in the 1950s!

In the later 1970s my wife and I decided to go in for the 'Goodlife', and my mother in Devon heard of someone who wanted to sell two colonies of bees. Spare beehives and equipment, and also new sheds were available, so a major expedition to the Westcountry was called for. We had at that time built a Mirror dinghy, and bought a trailer to tow it about, and I felt this might be the answer, so we travelled west with the trailer on the roof of the Hillman Hunter estate car.

The journey down to Devon wasn't too bad, and we then went to buy the shed which was destined to become a chicken house. Mounting this on the boat trailer was not an easy task, but luckily in its side it fitted within the wheels, and with several

Early Days on the Open Road

Transporting two colonies of bees in a hen house. Pit stop at Salisbury c 1978.

ropes was made as secure as possible. We then loaded my mother's unwanted bee equipment, and went off in search of the bees.

As anticipated, this proved to be the trickiest part of the operation, as it was not the best time of year to be moving them, and getting them into the shed, and properly secured, was a problem, not helped by a lack of co-operation on the part of the bees. However, it was done at last, and we set off back to Sussex, with many a backward glance into the wing mirrors to see if we were trailing a large cloud of bees behind us. In the end the journey was quite uneventful, though taken at a very gentle pace, and we had lots of eggs and honey as reward for this slightly audacious bit of cargo carrying.

A number of years later I was still a bee keeper, and had to make a move to Suffolk. It was mid-summer, not the best time, but I borrowed a pick up truck, and with the help of a good friend and fellow bee keeper, Peter, we halved my three strong hives and loaded them in the back, with a cover over them. At about 11.30pm we set off on our journey, Peter wearing his bee keeping overall with the hood down.

We had an excellent journey, M23, M25, A12 and were coming to the outskirts of Ipswich at 2.30am when I looked in my mirror and saw a huge police car right on my tail. I knew what was going to happen, suddenly all his lights blazed, 'Stop', 'Police', 'Pull Over', and all the rest, though he didn't use his siren.

I stopped and got out. The young policeman was on his own, and I think he must have had a bad night. 'Where have you come from?'

'From mid Sussex, Officer,' I said.

'Where are you going to?'

'Not far now,' I replied. 'Nearly to Woodbridge.'

'What have you got in the back?'

'I'll ask my friend Peter, who is dressed to do it, to show you' I replied. 'In the back we have about three hundred thousand bees, and they will be pretty angry, because they don't like any sort of travel, even at night. With your permission I will walk a quarter of a mile up the road while Peter obliges you, oh! One other thing. I should turn off that mobile lighting display on your car if I were you. Nothing will excite the bees so much as seeing that lot flashing.'

You have never seen a policeman get into his car and drive away so swiftly!

A restored Austin 10 with hamper basket on the carrier at the rear.

Chapter 16

DELIVERING THE GOODS

Two Model T Ford vans pose with the staff outside Beaumonts the butchers in Markyate c 1920.

While the private motorist might scratch his head, wondering how to load a grandfather clock into his MG sports car, there had always been others down the centuries whose work was the delivery of goods. You can imagine the scene centuries ago on Salisbury Plain, as a wiry little Welshman with a note tablet addresses the chief Druid.

'Is this Salisbury Plain, bach? I have some rocks to be delivered to Stonehenge, so it is.'

Rollers came to be replaced with wheels, and the horse, as we know, gave place to steam and the internal combustion engine. For centuries local communities, whether towns or villages, were largely self sufficient, with the occasional visit from a pedlar to supply what couldn't be made locally.

In the twentieth century this changed, and households in town and country came to rely more and more on 'imported' supplies. As this coincided with the coming of motor vehicles, the delivery van was the logical development. The van had signifi-

cant advantages. It was faster, and had a good, secure, load carrying capacity, with goods protected from the weather. The driver was also protected for the most part, as well. Loading and unloading was relatively easy through the rear doors, and the floor height aided lifting. The acquisition of a van was certainly a source of pride for a business, as the picture below shows, and indicated a 'go ahead' attitude in the business concerned.

Meat would have been quite a heavy item to carry about, so a van would be a great help to bring it from slaughterhouse to the butcher, and then to deliver it to customers. A large household with servants in the 1920s would have consumed a considerable quantity of meat in a week.

In the picture above we see the staff in their traditional garb, and there also appears to be a butchers' bicycle, unless that is a customer just arriving on the right.

In the days of horse-drawn carts and vans, the name of the owner was always displayed on the

Early Days on the Open Road

Robert Ellicott with his butcher's van in High Bickington, Devon, in 1925.

sides, and the new motor vans had even bigger advantages as mobile advertisement boards for the business. The name and nature of the business could be prominently displayed, and when the telephone came into general use the phone number of the business could also be given.

In our situation in Devon our butcher was Mr Lang, from the neighbouring village, and he drove a late 1930s Ford Van which he used as a mobile butcher's shop of a kind. The meat would be laid out in heaps around the back of the van, with some items like rabbits and half sheep hanging from hooks on the sides. Nearest the door was a wooden chopping block or operating table, whichever way one wanted to look at it, and there Mr Lang would trim some of the fat off his meat.

The moment he arrived in the village, the village dogs would gather round his van. There seemed to be some sort of order about this ritual, in that the dog whose home was being supplied with meat got the best position to catch a piece of flying fat thrown over Mr Lang's shoulder. The human customers learned to keep out of the way, or duck quickly. Standing chatting with your mouth open could result in you receiving a very unwanted and unappetising addition to your meat ration, as well as depriving a dog of its dinner!

Mr Lang was a very distinctive character, rather florid and sweaty, and always dressed in an old brown coat that had seen better days. He was kindly if in the mood, and would skin our rabbits for us with amazing dexterity. When he had finished dispensing our meat ration he would exchange a few words with mother about the weather, and then climb carefully into his van. He used to interest us because he always re-started the van by running it down the hill, and then letting in the clutch when it had gathered speed. The engine always started with a considerable roar, and we used to stand out in the lane to listen to his departing noises. I often wondered whether his van had a self starter at all, but of course it did, Mr Lang was just saving his battery.

By the time I came on the scene most households had given up baking their own bread, - perhaps the introduction of wartime rationing made it too difficult. Thus the bakers van had also become a regular visitor to the village, and again this van tended to operate as a mobile shop with a variety of loaves of bread on offer, as well as the Devon 'Tuffs', the equivalent of soft rolls anywhere else.

In our case, we had two bakers vans, and mother tried to divide her custom equally, on the basis that you didn't want to offend one of the delivery men in case the other went bust! One was from the Co-op, and was rather a large, sedate van, with a driver who was very efficient but not very friendly.

The other van came from the bakery in the next village, Staverton, and belonged to Ernie Medland.

When Motoring Was Fun

Kimpton, Baker and Confectioner of Woolmer Green, Herts, owned this van, and Margaret Green is showing it off in about 1930.

Charles Tuck and his daughter Cherri with his bakery van in Sculthorpe, Norfolk, in the 1930s. The van advertises 'Bride Cakes', complete with picture.

The Mac Fisheries shop in Blandford Forum, Dorset c.1940.

This was a small green Ford Eight van, which suited Ernie as he was rather small as well, and struggled to carry a large basket full of bread. But what fascinated us most was the inscription on the side: 'Ernie Medland and his Band' it proclaimed. Known as 'Ernie and the Swingers' the band travelled around in the van, empty of its usual cargo but still smelling deliciously of bread. In the picture above we see exactly the type of basket the bakers lugged around.

The next van that came to us was of more interest to the village cats than the dogs, as it was from Mac Fisheries! Fish came to our villages in two conditions, raw or cooked with chips!

The Mac Fisheries fish always had a distinctive smell, and especially on hot summers days, but the vans carried a good selection, and for many it was a case of Hobson's Choice, as far as fish supply was concerned.

The Fish and Chip van was a different matter. Each village would have its allocated time during the week, - I can even now remember that ours was 7pm on a Thursday night. The van would arrive, sounding its horn at intervals down the village street, and then take up station in the square. Both Mr and Mrs Chips would then attend to their friers, which must have been powered by bottled gas, and finally when all was ready the hatch would be opened by sliding across the glass door, and a hand bell would be rung, - which was quite unnecessary, as a considerable queue would already have formed

Two photographs showing the development of the Mac Fisheries Fish delivery team, from sign-written bicycles to a 1920s van, and then a neat little 1930s Morris van with patriotic flag. The scene is Blandford Forum in Dorset

by this time, including some of the ever hopeful village dogs, and even a bolder cat or two.

Horns and bells were quite superfluous down wind, as the delicious smell of fish and chips wafted through the village, and even those who had already decided on bangers and mash could be moved to change their minds at the last minute. Fi-nally this transport of delight would shut its window, everyone having been served, and go on its way leaving a very happy and well filled community.

The grocers mainly used their vans for bringing in supplies in bulk, and for making deliveries to customers. In our own situation mother would

When Motoring Was Fun

Vans belonging to Orme's the Grocers in Bakewell, Derbyshire, lined up for inspection in 1929.

phone the International Stores on a Monday morning to give our weekly order, and it would be delivered by a nice man driving a Morris Commercial van on the Wednesday afternoon. If we were out, the two boxes of groceries would be left on the back doorstep, neatly tied up with string, and the delivery man would take away the empty cardboard boxes left out for him, to be used again next time.

In Bakewell, for example, Orme's the grocers established a thriving business, with groceries and wines and spirits, almost like a modern day supermarket. They expanded so much that they were even permitted to demolish the 17th Century Hall in the square, to build new premises. They also established branches as far away as Sheffield, Derby, Stoke and Stafford.

To keep this flourishing business going they used a fleet of delivery vans, some of which are seen below. These were large vans, which could not only be used for making deliveries but also for bring in supplies, and delivering in bulk to the various stores. The vans in the picture below, all dating from the 1920s, appear to be an Albion on the right, and two others of the same make which I can't identify. They must have done a considerable mileage in a year!

Another interesting van from earlier in the 1920s is this one belonging to W.J. Guest. This van is interesting as Mr Guest describes himself as a 'Farm Produce Dealer' so perhaps was a sort of mobile Farm Shop in today's terms. It also appears that there is a phone number advertised on the van at the back.

Guest's 'Farm Produce Dealer' van with passenger Wilfred Taylor, in Loddiswell, Devon, in about 1920.

A few vans were actually fitted out as travelling grocery shops, and here we see one (opposite) from the early 1920s, with a housewife equipped with large basket plucking up the courage to tackle the rather inadequate steps to the shop floor! The van appears to have a lady driver/shop manager, who is preparing to do business, carrying her money bag.

In the top picture opposite the poultry dealer is aloft trying to extract the desired hen which must have been very well ventilated after a lively drive. Two customers appear to be already cuddling their chosen birds, and the original caption notes that the dealer was often able to offer his customers really new laid eggs, though if the road was rough they might be already scrambled!

An enterprising poultry dealer transports his birds in the 1920s.

A travelling Grocer's Shop from the early 1920s.

When Motoring Was Fun

A travelling Grocery Van in Stithians, Cornwall, about 1930.

The travelling grocer's van shown above belonged to Mr Phillips of Stithians, and was based on the chassis of a six cylinder Chevrolet car, which was a well known and ideal foundation for many such vehicles worldwide.

It was fitted out with shelves, so that again the many items on offer can be seen through the side windows. It also had a special feature, in the form of a large tank of paraffin slung beneath the body. In an age where many people cooked and lit their houses with paraffin cookers and lamps this was a welcome source of replenishment. We used to have special cans to keep the paraffin in when not in use. Paraffin cookers always had a very distinctive smell, which was not entirely conducive to a good appetite!

Two other slogans on this transport of delight for the housewife read 'We study to please the customer' and 'Personal service satisfies.' I wonder who thought those up!

The other business that made daily deliveries to us was the dairy, or perhaps a farm, bringing the morning milk. The milk float dates from the 1930s, but dairies also had more usual vans, as we see from the picture of Jane's Corner Dairy, in Brixham, below, with their Morris 8 Van parked outside. This dairy, as was appropriate in Devon, advertised 'Cream by Post' and I can imagine the cream, with a golden crust on the top, waiting to go on top of a scone with a good dollop of home made strawberry jam. I think I shall have to pause to collect myself!

Then there were a host of specialist vans. Here we see two unusual examples. The Jesty family of Spetisbury had a farm with water cress beds, and used their van to take their produce to the nearest railway station. The imposing van was a 1923 Humber, and the picture dates from 1929.

Opposite is shown the The Bridport Gas Company had their first van, a second hand Trojan, in 1932, and it is seen here with two men and a dog! Presumably it was used for supplying fittings and doing repairs, and was not actually filled with gas, or people would have given it a very wide berth!

If one had to be careful with van loads of foodstuffs or gas, one could be more robust with carpets and linoleums. But the company of Marks Bros of Wellington, like many others, offered House Removals, and that was a very different matter. You

The Humber Van belong to the Jesty family of Spetisbury, in Dorset, used to deliver their water cress crop to the railway at Bailey Gate c.1929.

Jane's Corner Dairy, King Street, Brixham, with Morris van in the 1930s.

A Marks Bros van from Wellington in the mid 1930s.

Trojan van used by the Bridport Gas Company in 1932.

could find yourself carrying all Mrs Nosworthy's precious china and glassware, and all under the very watchful eye of the good housewife herself. She will have packed it all herself, distaining offers of help, but woe betide you if a single glass is cracked when she comes to unpack, for nothing you can say or do will absolve you from blame!

House removals were usually done with a larger van, but either way packing was like doing a huge three-dimensional jigsaw puzzle, and the vans car-

ried a wealth of straps and blankets, with struts along the sides to which items of furniture could be lashed to prevent movement during the journey. My experience of the men who did this job is that they were always unbelievably skilled at their trade.

The other group of specialist vans in those days belonged to the Post Office, and came in three kinds. First, the small vans used by postmen to deliver the letters morning and afternoon, and to clear the letter boxes. My earliest memories are of Morris 8 vans, a few of the older mid Thirties models, and then the van based on the series Y, with headlights set on to the front wings. These were a

Richard Tucker's Post Bus preparing to leave Bridport, for Beaminster, Dorset, in 1925.

'Creamax' ice cream delivered by motorcycle in Haughley, Suffolk c.1935.

very common sight as they buzzed round all day. The second group were larger vans used for bulk deliveries of letters from sorting offices to railway stations to catch the mail train, or for parcels deliveries. The arrival of one of these vans at the front gate always caused excitement. They tended to be the larger Morris Commercial vans, with the small circular windows in the back doors. I had a much cherished Dinky Toy model of one.

Finally, and less often seen, were the Post Office Telephones vans. These tended to be the same models, I think Morris must have had a virtual monopoly for supplying the Post Office vans at this period. The interesting feature was the way these little vans were fitted out as mobile workshops, with their access ladders carried on the roof. They also carried a step ladder inside, and pruning equipment to sort out over enthusiastic tree branches which interfered with the overhead telephone lines. Incidentally, climbing a telephone pole, and working at the top, held in place with a leather strap, involved a good deal of skill and not a little courage. Not for the faint hearted!

Later, in the 1950s, the Morris Minor van proved to be the ideal vehicles for both Royal mail and the Telephones, and these excellent vans remained in use for many years giving wonderful service.

In the olden times the travelling tinker and pedlar would announce their arrival with their distinctive street cries. In my youth we listened out for the chimes of the ice cream van! At first, during the war and soon after, the van was a rarity. But gradually they multiplied, first sponsored by either Walls or Lyons, and they just carried the usual selection of ices in a deep freeze in the van, and powered off a generator. Gradually the selection became greater, with vans which supplied soft ice cream in cornets, very difficult to manage on a hot summer's day without getting ice cream dripping along your arm and off your elbow!

I have closed the chapter with a typical village scene from the 1950s, a scene I know today. The delivery van, a Morris J Type, dates from the early 1950s, and had a forward control driving position, with the driver sitting beside and above the engine. This was not always cool or comfortable, but gave a much greater carrying capacity than the older Model Y.

Thousands of these vans were delivered for Royal Mail duties in the 1950s, as well as telephones and many other tasks. The setting of the one in the picture is very typical, but I always felt the designer missed a trick when he made a radiator which gave the van such a 'hangdog' expression!

A Morris delivery van, of on the Green at Haughley in Suffolk, 1950s.

Chapter 17

PASSENGER COMFORT AND REFRESHMENT

Enterprising villagers entice passing motorists with the temptations of tea, Coc-Cola and and cigarettes, sometime in the late 1930s, location unknown. A Morris 8 tourer in the foreground.

We have already noted that the earliest cars gave their drivers and passengers little personal comfort and poor protection from inclement weather. You would very likely arrive at your destination either wet, or dusty, or if it was a day of 'sunshine and showers' you could be coated in mud! Seats could be pretty basic, made of wood or metal, with but meagre padding. You had to hang on to whatever was handy to avoid being thrown out.

This state of affairs was rapidly improved on the more luxurious cars, with an enclosed interior along the lines of the best horse drawn carriages. The arrival of better cars tempted their owners to become more ambitious with regard to the length and speed of journeys. You could now do in a single day what the old coach and horses could only manage in three. But you still had to make pit stops for the comfort of your passengers.

The genteel Tea Room at the roadside could be an ideal spot in the afternoon, and though one usually associates such a visit with sitting out in the garden in the sunshine guzzling those cream scones, the picture below reminds us that it could be a winter experience with hot muffins and a roaring fire in the grate.

It would be difficult to drag oneself away and face the rigours of the open road again after such a delightful tea.

There were other rigours of the road that were not even acknowledged in genteel circles. After the bone-shakers of the 1920s, the trend was towards softer springing, and as a result a generation of cars in the 1950s rolled most horribly on bends, and at that point most roads had plenty for them to roll around. We did not have seat belts, and if three people sat on the back seat they all swayed together! Many a motorist, especially the father of the

133

When Motoring Was Fun

A party of gentlemen from Bridport, Dorset, stop for refreshments at the Blue Ball Inn, Salway Ash, in the 1920s.

family, carried several bowls of one description or another, and it was a common sight to see a car stopped by the side of the road with one or two junior passengers being parted from the ample cream tea they had eaten an hour earlier.

I know of one family in the later 1950s whose summer holiday always had to be taken in a seaside town about 25 miles from their home, because that was the limit of endurance for most of the children in the car. Luckily the seaside town in question, Southwold, was utterly delightful, so they actually enjoyed a much better holiday than might have been experienced 200 miles from home.

Then there was the need for another kind of pit stop. My mother, reared by strict Victorian parents, always employed a number of euphemisms for the word 'lavatory'. Out on the open road, they became Yellow signs, darling.' I can remember the relief in her voice as the old Hillman Minx ploughed slowly towards Salisbury. 'Only five miles to go now, darlings, and we shall be at the Yellow Sign in Wilton.'

She carried a most essential mental map of the countries roads, with all the yellow signs marked, which was a great relief to us all.

Sometimes, out in remote rural areas, the looked for signs just did not exist. I remember a trip to North Cornwall, when we had failed to find the Yellow Sign in Tavistock, I think it was shut for repairs or something, and we drove on to Gracestone Bridge across the river Tamar in increasing desperation. Beside the bridge mother pulled into the small lay-by, and as we piled out she announced 'Boys up river, girls down river,' and led the female contingent at the trot along the fisherman's path.

No other directions were necessary, and when we all met up again by the car we were a much happier family!

When it came to stopping for meals, the situation was very different to today. Now there is a 'Little Chef' or the equivalent ever few miles along the larger roads, or you can turn aside into a village, often following a sign, and find a delightful Inn offering a menu that would put a London restaurant to shame.

In those far off days of the mid twentieth century it was not like that. You could indeed find a hotel or a restaurant before too long, but a meal there would cost you a good deal of money, and, perhaps more important, take a good deal of time. You did not really want a head waiter fussing over you and proffering the wine list when there was still a long journey ahead.

You could of course find a lovely local pub, like the Blue Ball Inn above. You could go in, and as long as the local brewery had topped up the cellar lately, the buxom barmaid would go on pulling you delicious pints of beer until the stuff came out of your ears. There was no question of 'Would you happen to be the driver of that there car out there, Zur?' or 'Do ye really feel another six for the road be a good thing, master?'.

But if you were to ask here for something to eat, she would be likely to make an interesting gesture in the direction of the large jar of pickled onions occupying pride of place on the bar, and bid you help yourself! It could be, that if you had chatted

Early Days on the Open Road

A beautiful if somewhat draughty picnic site in 1964. Dartmoor, Devon.

away for an hour or so, and paid her a number of compliments ('I love the way your muscles ripple when you pull me another pint') then she might be persuaded to go into the rear part of the establishment and create you a cheese sandwich. This would consist of two thick hunks of homemade bread, giving it a total thickness of about three inches, with a small sliver of 'mousetrap' cheese hidden deep within its depths.

So what was the solution? Well, you carried your refreshments with you, and probably also carried a picnic basket. Every newly wedded couple were presented with one as a wedding present. It would have compartments for your cutlery, and sections where the cups and plates were held in by straps. So all you had to do was chose a nice place, and in those days the sun always shone, and there was always a gate open into a newly mown field, with space for the children to play. We never saw a fly or a wasp in those days, and no farmer suddenly appeared with a 12-bore shotgun and three ferocious dogs to evict us from our paradise!

As already chronicled, in 1954 my mother decided on her return visit to Austria, and my father generously allowed her to go without him, on condition that she took all the children with her! Very early on we discovered that my mother had an unsuspected problem, the need to make a pit stop about every forty miles or so, in order to brew up a cup of tea!

We carried with us, as on the 1930s trip, the family picnic basket. This I suspect was of Edwardian vintage, so beginning to show its age. It was a wicker basket, with all the usual compartments for tea and sugar, crockery and cutlery. It also had a small metal tripod, and a metal kettle which perched on the top. Underneath this rather unstable contraption was inserted a methylated spirit burner, to heat the kettle. There cannot have been any other heating equipment in the history of the world which produced more fumes and smoke, and less heat!

All the way across France mother sought out little rural lay-bys, or cart tracks, and then fired up her infernal machine, while we, her loyal and supportive children moved as far away as possible, pretending that we were nothing to do with this smoky example of English custom.

But finally, mother met her match. The Land Rover was climbing nimbly up the pass between Switzerland and Austria when we came to a small lay-by on the left of the road. It was one of those with a low wall, and if you went and looked over the wall it was a sheer drop of several thousand feet to a lake below. In the lay-by was parked a van, which announced that it belonged to Mr Higgins, Plumber, of Hackney.

One back door of the van was open, and smoke billowed forth. Seeing a fellow English tourist, and one possibly in distress, excited us all, and we pulled over into the lay-by and stopped behind the van. As we got out and stood around, the van continued to smoke, but there was no other sign of life. We coughed, and talked loudly to attract attention to ourselves, and suddenly Mr Higgins put his head out of the door and said

''Ullo, you English then?'

'Yes,' we replied, 'We just stopped to look at the view.' And then as the smoke appeared to increase, 'We saw the smoke and wondered if you were alright?'

'Oh, fine, fine,' said Mr. Higgins. ' I said to Mrs Higgins this morning, Mother, I said, I'm fed up with this Continental Breakfast stuff. What say we go up the pass. I got some nice swine's flesh and a few eggs, and we'll light up the old Primus and have a real good fry-up.'

And that is exactly what he was doing, a stranger in a foreign land, and it really smelled utterly delicious!

On arrival at mother's favourite Inn, in the village of Pettneu in the Austrian Tirol, her one great need was for tea. We spoke no Austrian, and they spoke no English, but mother managed to make her needs known by means of gestures. Then Maria arrived, bearing a huge tray loaded with white

An early AA road sign.

A wayside hut at Newton Poppleford, Devon, serving, among a host of other things, tea and refreshments for passing motorists.

crockery, and there were lots of smiles as she withdrew, and mother began to inspect the tea tray.

There was a huge white teapot, a jug of hot water, bowl of sugar, bowl of lemon slices, lots of cups, but no milk. Instead, there was a jug of what looked like rather thin gravy. A conference was held, but as we did not know the way to the kitchen, or the word for milk, there seemed little we could do. Mother poured tea into each cup, added lemon and sugar where desired, and then almost absentmindedly added a tot of gravy. We sipped cautiously, then with increasing enthusiasm. It was absolutely delicious. Cups were passed for a refill, and by the time we had finished there was not a drop of liquid left on the tray!

Mother brewing up in the Land Rover at Amiens Station, 1954.

For the next few days, tea time became the climax of the day, the one thing not to be missed at any price. Would we do a trip down to Innsbruck? Only if we could be sure to be back in time for tea! Unfortunately for younger members of the party, my dear Godmother, who had come to give moral support to my mother, and who had been on the original trip in the 1930s, was very conscientious and tried to apply her Austrian phrasebook whenever possible, and about the fourth day she had become fluent enough to inquire what was in the gravy jug.

'Ah yes' responded Frau Matt, 'it is a special liquid which is brewed by the monks in their monastery up the mountain behind. It is called Cognac.' After that tea time reverted to its usual boring self, with plenty of milk and no gravy!

The return journey in the Land Rover across Switzerland and France mirrored the journey out, and in due course we came to the city of Amiens, and mother was desperate for a cup of tea. She pulled into the car park at 'La Gare' and retired to the back to fire up the picnic basket.

Although it was raining quite heavily, we, her loyal children, abandoned her and took shelter under the awning of the local Patisserie. Soon smoke began to issue from the back of the Land Rover, and we watched in fascination as two enormous Gendarmes, resplendent in cloaks and peaked caps, marched across to the car swinging their batons, to see what 'Les fou Anglais' were up to now.

It is greatly to my mother's credit that not only did she talk her way out of it, in rather indifferent French, but she nearly got them to accept a cup of tea!

In the 1960s traffic jams to the Westcountry became so problematic that tourists could be held up for hours at just one spot. Here the police have set up a refreshment point to cater for tired and hungry motorists near Exeter.

A chapter on comfort and refreshment for the occupants of our Transports of Delight would not be complete without a reference to the places where they could stay the night, or perhaps stay a week, along the road. We have looked at the wayside Inn, but Britain could offer the weary traveller every kind of accommodation, and sometimes some very surprising jewels could be found in very remote places.

The Automobile Association had become a large and most comprehensive organisation by the end of the 1930s, and together with the RAC provided much advice and help to car travellers of every description. The photograph of Honiton on page 40 reveals all sorts of roadside signs to aid motorists, including AA and RAC signs. The AA Hotel Handbook for 1939 was produced just before war broke out, and motoring was never quite the same again.

It begins by defining a hotel, according to the Oxford English Dictionary, as 'a house for entertainment of strangers and travellers.' The book, which runs to 623 pages, goes on to describe the origin of the AA and to note that they have provided nearly 100 000 traffic signs 'for the guidance and protection of road users.' (I don't think my mother's Yellow Sign in Wilton was one of them, actually, it was more for the relief of road users!).

The AA classified hotels with a one to five star rating, and such classified hotels could be recognised by the AA lamp or sign exhibited outside the premises. A five star hotel would be exceptionally large, luxurious and well appointed. Three star would have 'the ordinary standard of excellence required by motorists, namely hotels where good food, hot meals daily, clean well furnished bedrooms and bathrooms and comfortable accommodation etc. can be relied on.'

One star were 'small hotels, where the catering and bedroom accommodation are limited, but satisfactory in other respects.' Many a motorist would quickly learn that small was often beautiful, and a great deal cheaper!

Location of course dictated the number of hotels in a given place, and two places well known to me are an interesting contrast. In Ilfracombe were to be found a four star hotel, three of three star rating, and four two star ones. There were also twenty-nine private hotels and guest houses. The top rate was 9 guineas a week. Ipswich, a much larger town, had two three star hotels and a guest house!

Chapter 18

TRANSPORT DELIGHTS FOR ALL

Passengers clutch their belongings and a horse rider reigns in nervously behind a very early charabanc type motor bus providing the first motor service from Llansteffan to Carmarthen, 1 May 1909.

In this instance the starting point is probably the Stage Coach, as there is no record of the Roman horse-drawn charabanc! Horse-drawn buses and trams developed mainly during the nineteenth century, and as usual the magazine *Punch* saw the funny side.

Horse Bus driver to very fat lady trying to get through the rear door of the conveyance:

'Try sideways, Mrs Jones, try sideways.'

Fat lady: 'Bless you, Jarge, I ain't got no zideways!'

The first motor vehicles to roam the streets of our towns were the electric trams. They generally took over from the horses in the last decade of the nineteenth century, but timing varied in different places. As we have seen, the concept of a small 'railway carriage' moving on rails along the street, with no power to steer or chose where it was going to was at times difficult for both motorists and pedestrians to cope with. There was also a good deal of experimenting. In Addiscombe, for example, the Norwood

District tramway was formed in 1882, using horse drawn trams. In 1883 the system was leased to the Steam Tramways Traction Co. but horses remained in use, and not a puff of steam was seen.

Several companies tried to run the trams, but though the horses figured splendidly in the local Horse Show, the companies went bust with regularity. Finally, on 1 January 1900, the British Electric Traction Company took over the tramway, and, appropriately, a new era began.

In the case of Croydon and Addiscombe, the trams were majestic and much admired, and their routes expanded to cover larger parts of the area. However, here as elsewhere the effect of the First World War was huge, and particularly in it's effect on manpower shortages, and lack of essential maintenance work. As early as 1919 there were discussions about what to do, and these dragged on until finally the last tram ran on the network on 31st March 1927. The following day buses moved in to serve the community.

Early Days on the Open Road

A tram making stately progress down the Lower Addiscombe Road, Croydon c.1920.

Tram 65 on the last day of trams in Addiscombe, 31 March 1927.

The tram has always been a most distinctive vehicle, with the rattle it makes crossing a points, and the scraping of the overhead conductor. Many had striking livery, and were much loved in their communities. Again Punch drew attention to the eccentricity of the tram and its passengers. An old lady is alighting from the tram and says to the conductor 'Is it safe for me to put my foot on the rail?' 'Quite safe' the conductor replies, 'as long as you don't put your other foot on the overhead wire!'

Bournemouth tramcar No.30 en route westward to Poole Park, Dorset, 1912.

The motor bus had several advantages over the tram, but in particular a greater speed, and the ability to go everywhere. However, many places which had trams hung on to them, as they had a special character and charm all their own. We now know that they were very environmentally friendly as well!

In Austria on a later visit than those mentioned, we stayed at a hotel in a small village up a valley, some ten miles or so from Innsbruck. There was a railway station in the village, and a small two car electric train left for the city at regular intervals, so we decided to go for a trip. When we got to the outskirts of Innsbruck, the two car train turned itself into a tram, and glided down the streets on tram rails, doing a large circuit and visiting the important places like the Town Hall and Railway station

A smiling driver and conductor stand proudly in front of their GWR motor bus at Sennen in Cornwall, heading for Land's End c.1920.

before finding its way back to its original track and heading for the peace of the mountains. You could almost hear it give a sigh of relief as it left the town behind.

It seemed such an excellent mode of transport to link town and countryside I am surprised that we have never done it over here.

The development of the motor bus, and its cousin the charabanc, owed a good deal to local initiative in the early years. As we have already seen some local carters were ready to fit improvised seating to large vans, or to make their own passenger carrying bodies to fit a lorry chassis. One garage proprietor in Halstead in Essex fitted a home made coach body to a Model T Ford chassis.

In the 1920s, following the First World War, many and varied bus companies came into existence. The railway companies, used to transporting people, saw the operation of buses as a logical extension of their networks in areas where the railway itself had not penetrated.

Most bus companies were based in a town or city and then served the surrounding district. Some might link two or three towns together. There was much swapping about, and takeovers and mergers.

In the following picture we see an open top double decker bus owned then by the Salisbury & District Motor Services Company. The year after, the company was taken over by the Wilts and

A Salisbury & District bus with driver and passengers posing at Wilton, 1920.

Dorset company in 1921. The following year a rival company, Victory Motor Services, challenged the monopoly, but in 1933 they also were bought out by Wilts and Dorset. The bus in the picture operated between Salisbury and Wilton, and was very popular but rather uncomfortable. Those wheels ensured a pretty bumpy ride for the passengers.

As the years passed, the bus manufacturers and operators looked for three improving qualities in their vehicles. The first was passenger carrying capacity, because this directly affected the revenue which each vehicle could generate. By reducing the size of seats, and making the best use of the available space, it became possible to get about 30 people into a single decker bus, and about 60 into a double decker, all of the passengers being under cover.

Early Days on the Open Road

A Garford Bus, as used by Miltons on the Crediton to Exeter run in the 1920s.

The second consideration was speed, so that vehicles could maintain a tight schedule, and give the best service possible, as well as the best income for the company.

The third factor was passenger comfort, and the provision of inflated tyres and better springing, as well as more comfortable seats went a long way towards achieving this.

In our village in Devon, with a population of about 200, we had a service of six buses a day most days. Three were Devon General red buses that took us via Ipplepen to Newton Abbot, and the other three Western National green buses that took us via Staverton station and Dartington to Totnes. During and after the war we used the buses a lot, as they ran at very convenient times, and a bus journey was much more fun than being crammed into the car. Just seeing who else was on the bus was most interesting, and then listening to the conversation in the seat behind you enabled you to catch up on a great deal of village news!

In the towns the open top buses gave way to enclosed models, and more frequent services, with increasing numbers of bus stops, were created.

For many people the development of bus services, with ever faster and more comfortable vehicles, brought about a huge change in their lives. Shopping and visiting the market in the local town, both to buy and sell, were part of the weekly routine, instead of a three times a year achievement. Bus fares were really very reasonable, and children had reduced fares, so family outings suddenly became a possibility. Buses could be quite adventurous too. I used to return to my godmothers house along the Devon coast from my first school in Dartmouth every day, and the great hope was that when we charged up the stairs on the double decker bus, the front seats would be vacant.

From this vantage point, as the bus headed west, we got the most superb view of land and sea, and it only added spice to our journey when one evening a part of the road slipped down the cliff into the sea a few hours after we had passed that way. Would it happen again? We wondered and hoped!

Meanwhile buses became more eye-catching, and local operators took great pride in having a really

Buses became prime sites for carrying adverts, as here in Hertfordshire c.1920.

When Motoring Was Fun

About 1900 this early motor bus charabanc has brought a party to the Land's End Hotel.

smart livery for their vehicles. There were a number of competing makers, of which Bedford, AEC, Leyland and Bristol were the leaders.

Hand in hand with the development of the buses were the charabancs, which would evolve into coaches. Here there was a different atmosphere. The bus might mean going to and from work or school, or doing the shopping. But the charabanc meant an outing, a holiday, some exotic and exciting destination, and one's best clothes!

In the picture above we see an amazing early charabanc from about 1900, with a huge awning over the entire top of the vehicle. At what speed the whole thing would have blown away we can only conjecture, but the vehicle cannot surely have exceeded walking pace, especially at a windy place like Land's End!

Again, looking closely, one is struck by the elegance of the clothes, as well as the impressive bodywork and very solid and unyielding tyres!

One of the most looked-for occasions was the works' outing, and it is obvious from the many photographs taken that it was considered obligatory to have a formal record of each occasion. The following images evoke the days when groups, clubs, church and chapel communities would set off by charabanc for a day's outing.

A party from Wilton sets of to visit Cheddar caves c.1930.

Early Days on the Open Road

The yearly men's outing to the seaside from Woolmer Green in the 1920s.

Men and women from Watchet in Somerset on a visit to Cheddar Caves c.1930.

Members of the church choir out for a day from Thatcham in Berkshire in the 1930s.

Pomery's charabanc about to set off from St Mawes for a day out in Cornwall c.1930.

When Motoring Was Fun

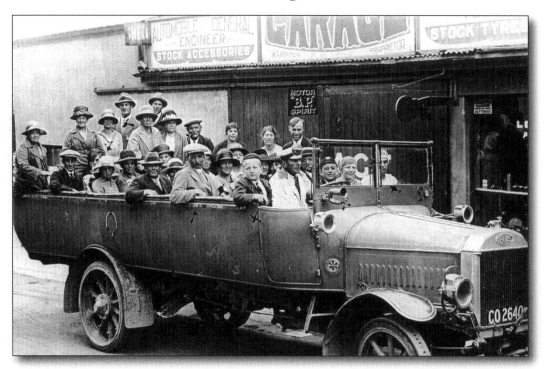

An outing from Northlew by charabanc, outside Okehampton Garage in about 1920.

The charabanc voyagers do not always look so cheerful in their formal photographs, and some look understandably decidedly apprehensive.

Jack Webber, from Northlew near Okehampton, went in to Plymouth regularly, and would take rabbits and chickens to sell in the market. On one occasion, just as he was packing up, he noticed a neighbouring stall was also packing up and selling off the remaining fruit cheap. Jack always had a eye for a bargain, so he bought a quantity of strawberries, and put them for safe keeping under his seat in the coach.

Unfortunately, on the journey, a child in the seat behind had a 'little accident' on the floor. Jack, however, was not a man to be deflected from his purpose by a small puddle of fate, and duly dried off his strawberries and sold the lot at a good profit on his return to Northlew. I expect his customers remarked on the delicious flavour of 'that there Plymouth fruit!'

The early charabanc was indeed a transport of delight for thousands of people, partly because it meant a trip to 'foreign parts' and partly because it truly represented a holiday excursion, a real break in the weekly round of work and more work. It must have been a cause of great excitement in the village or town when the great day arrived, and the charabanc wheezed into the market square, to be greeted by a large party all turned out in their Sunday best.

On these outings the all important driver acted often as conductor and guide as well, and a good driver with a lot of local knowledge and plenty of ready wit could greatly enliven an outing for all concerned. Some of the drivers were supplied with a smart uniform to wear, in order to demonstrate their rank and importance! As noted, the coaches travelled at a very sedate speed, and being quite high off the road offered views over hedges not often glimpsed, as well as views into other people's property which were a source of great interest! In addition to this the seats were of the bench type variety, with each row of seats having it's own door, so that there could be a lot of manoeuvring to make sure that you sat next to the travelling companion of your special choice, usually a member of the opposite sex!

In the evening the charabanc would rumble gently back to the village, and in the darkness and chill of the twilight, many an arm would be slipped round a pair of slim shoulders, to prevent a lady occupant from being thrown about by violent cornering!

The three ingredients for a perfect day out, for the male members of the party in particular, would be wine, women and song! During the course of the days excursion regular visits to local hostelries would be essential. The gentlemen sampled the local beers, and the ladies were permitted to drink a soft drink or cider, which was always considered suitable. As the cider often had a higher alcoholic content than the beer, the lovely ladies of the party grew ever more pliable as the day progressed.

Early Days on the Open Road

A party leaves the Clarence Hotel, Seaton, in a Lancia open-top coach in about 1926.

Then there was the song. There were many old and traditional songs like 'Widecombe Fair' and 'Green Grow the Rushes O' and the best singers in the party would usually occupy the back seat to stimulate others to join in. The actual songs chosen demanded some care and tact, and would much depend on the nature of the outing. If it was the annual outing of the village Rugby Club or the Farm Labourers Union, then the singing would be lusty and quite uninhibited, and the content of songs much given to describing interesting and improbable entanglements between the sexes. If however, it was the village children's outing, or the choir or bellringers, and the vicar was sitting beside the driver in the front seat of the charabanc, then songs of a much more seemly nature would be chosen, with even the odd popular hymn. There could even be an accompaniment on a harmonica, if the road was not too bumpy.

During the twenties and thirties the same progress in coach design was seen as with the buses, with the emphasis on the comfort of passengers. Coach companies would be aware of the attraction of the latest model for potential customers, and coaches would be painted in eye catching liveries, and with the proprietors name and telephone number clearly displayed.

The essential feature was still to pack as many passengers in as possible, in reasonable comfort, and yet keep the overall size of the vehicle manageable, as it might often have to navigate quite narrow village streets and lanes as it took its happy occupants to the sea side. One design improvement was to site the engine beneath the floor, and give the driver a forward control position. This both gave him excellent visibility, and also enabled half a dozen extra passengers to be accommodated on the coach. The picture below shows the progress in design to about 1960, with a more streamlined front to the vehicle on the right compared to the much older Bedford coaches on the left.

Coach outings have always been popular either as day trips, or for longer holidays, roaming all over Europe. But the gradual change in car ownership after about 1960 meant that there was no longer quite the same mystique about such outings.

There was one other feature of the traditional outing, for the old coaches carried no toilet facilities, and the occupants intake of beer could be remarkable, putting a strain on all the passengers. It would be a common sight, especially after dusk, to find the Village Outing coach pulled into a conveniently large lay-by, and a long line of the male occupants helpfully irrigating the nearby hedge, each ignoring his companions, and with a look of studied concentration on his face!

Chapter 19

CHANGING ROADS AND GROWING CONGESTION

High Street, Honiton, in the 1960s is beginning to show signs of the traffic congestion that has blighted all our towns a cities since. Note the two policemen on traffic duty.

Sadly, and almost inevitably, the motor car became the victim of its own outstanding success. In the narrow streets of towns, and along inadequate winding main roads and twisting country lanes, there were just too many cars. Even if you accomplished your journey with relative ease, you then faced the problem of where to park your car.

As more and more people could afford a car, the number of car owners with garages diminished. No longer did every car owner sweep through wrought iron front gates, ease gently down the gravelled drive, and draw up in front of the garage block. Now many a car owner drove slowly and with increasing panic down a narrow street bordered on each side by Terrace houses, looking for a gap along the roadside big enough to squeeze his Mini into.

When I first arrived in Ipswich, driving the family Land Rover, I discovered that the gap between my landlady's semi-detached and the next couple of houses was just big enough to squeeze the Land Rover into. But alas, you did not have room to open the doors more than six inches, and even then I

was quite large! But the Land Rover was extremely versatile. If you unlaced the back of the canvas hood, and then drove into the gap, folded down the passenger seat and clambered over into the back, you could then climb out over the tailboard and re-lace the hood flap, giving as much security as a Land Rover ever had. It did however look slightly odd to passing pedestrians and neighbours across the road to watch me drive carefully into the gap, and then a minute or two later emerge stern first from beneath the canvas at the back. Being British, nobody ever commented on this strange procedure!

It was, as we have seen, the towns and cities of our land which felt the first problems, and sometimes acutely. Narrow streets with substantial buildings restricted space, while the shopping areas and other attractions drew in cars like bees to a honeycomb. Some provided 'out of town' car parks, but the problems of congestion multiplied. The picture on the following page gives a vivid foretaste of what was to come. The setting is the General Strike in

Early Days on the Open Road

Traffic jams were already a feature of London roads in the late 1920s.

London in 1926, and with most of the capital's buses strike bound, many brought their cars into the city with predictable results. This is the scene (above) on the Embankment as all the city financiers tried to get to their desks at the same time. Once they got to the office, if they succeeded in arriving at all, they would then have spent much of the day trying to park.

The powers that be tackled this problem with zest. Apart from bypasses and mazes of one-way streets, they devised an incredibly complicated system of parking places, monitored by parking meters, which in turn were monitored by Traffic Wardens, the best loved of all the motorist's friends, until the arrival of the wheel clamping parasite.

Policemen were put on traffic duty, to help the motorist. (This was before they were put into cars, and given cameras to boost Police funds!). In the picture of Honiton I can see two constables supervising the busy scene.

Policeman did not always speed up the traffic, and as mentioned, the centre of Ipswich being a very busy four crossroads was especially slow, which could lead to problems.

Doctor Bunt driving along Tavern Street in the direction of his home had been out visiting a string of patients, had accepted several cups of tea against his better judgement, and was dying for a pee. At last his queue of traffic began to move, but just as he reached the head of the line, up went the policeman's hand with great authority, and he was forced again to stop and wait.

But the poor doctor was desperate, and looking round he espied a length of rubber tubing and a funnel on his back seat, which had been intended for an equally desperate patient but not employed. By his right foot was a small inspection hatch in the floor, to check the fluid level in the brake master cylinder. A few moments, and some basic plumbing later, and the flood of relief for the doctor was immense. He had just finished operations, when the policeman turned and waved him on.

He moved forward, almost singing with joy, but to his horror the policeman's hand again went up, and then when he stopped, the officer came round to his car window.

'Excuse me for stopping you, sir,' he said 'but are you aware that your radiator appears to be leaking badly?'

'Ah yes' replied the flustered doctor, 'yes, officer, it often does that!' and he drove off as quickly as traffic permitted.

London always led the way in congestion, and it is interesting to remember that in my little 1954 Hillman Husky, sidevalve engine and a very gentle performance, I could always drive from the centre of Ipswich to Big Ben in exactly two hours on a Sunday night. You would never do it in that time now, without breaking every speed limit. That is because now there are about one hundred and thirty sets of traffic lights, I counted them on a journey in about 1994, though I do have to admit that some have been removed by a new road since then, and also you didn't have to drive vast distances to get round Witham and Chelmsford and such like places.

Out on the main roads of the country progress was usually better, but the standard of lorry driving had slipped badly, so that lorries would make no effort to help cars to pass them, but rather seemed to do everything possible to prevent such a happening, by driving in the middle of the road and breaking their speed limits.

Only the other day I found myself applying again the Tyler rule for Sanity on the Road, after having followed a speeding truck for a number of miles on a twisting main road. 'When the dirty and swaying backside of the lorry in front finally becomes utterly tedious, take the first turning on the left.' We did, and immediately were engulfed by a quiet, beautiful Yorkshire lane, which led us on, pixie fashion, to a perfect place to stop and have a picnic lunch. The sun shone, a little, the birds sang,

When Motoring Was Fun

In pre-war days, most villages, like quiet Brundall in Norfolk, saw few cars, and local bus services provided a regular means of travel for most.

and when we eventually rejoined the main road the lorry was nowhere to be seen! It is a procedure that has never failed me these last fifty years.

Of course, I would be dishonest if I did not admit that you can also become the victim of congestion while travelling down a country lane as well. It may be a herd of cows or a flock of sheep, in no great hurry to go anywhere. It may be that a tree has fallen across the road, and is being cut up. If the combine harvester is too wide to go through a gateway, an interesting jam will develop until such time as the offending gateway has been demolished and the quiet pace of rural life resumes.

Then there are notable country events which will draw a crowd along a totally inadequate road. Village fetes, point-to-point horse races, sightings of rare birds, even, as we have seen, wrecked sailing ships, will all do the trick. There is no scope for turning round and trying another route, so you switch off your engine, and just sit there enjoying the bird song. The shared adventure breeds the usual British camaraderie, and total strangers will converse with one another, in a most uninhibited way, and speculate together on the cause of the delay.

In the following picture we see the exact thing happening, as cars stop trying to get to Braemar, in Scotland, and pause for thought. They may be heading for the Highland Games, but for the moment drivers and passengers have stopped, climbed

The winding road to Braemar, Scotland, and a queue of cars in the 1920s.

out of their cars, and are talking to one another and admiring the marvellous scenery.

Another feature of the changing roads is the signs. In the old days they were largely informative, giving directions or warning of dangerous corners, and one knew how to use them to advantage, Even the rare 'Single track road with passing places' could be a pleasure, as one dashed from one passing place to the next, willing there not to be another vehicle doing the same thing in the opposite direction.

'Beware of Low Flying Aircraft' always seemed a bit pointless, after all if you were hit by a low flying aircraft while at the wheel of your car there was precious little you could do. However, now it reminds

Early Days on the Open Road

West Street, Fareham, at the end of the 1950s, with lots of vehicles and some road works!

me of Brockbank's lovely cartoon of the speeding jeep with three military occupants who have taken off on a hump backed bridge, and are flying a lot higher than the 'low flying aircraft' which is just passing, and about which they have been warned!

Other animal and natural hazards one is also powerless to avoid. The jumping deer does indeed do just that , as I know to our cost, - which was considerable! Could not a notice be put up for the deer, 'Busy road, do not cross.'?

Then there are the rocks that are going to fall on you. It does not help to spend your time craning your head to look out of the windscreen at the cliff above, as you will then crash into an oncoming car, which will do more damage than the rock would have done.

And what do you do about giant ducks or toads, which will leap upon your vehicle and squash it, or even lay eggs on it? It all becomes very worrying for the innocent and peace loving motorist.

In the photograph above we see Fareham before all the yellow lines were painted and zebra crossings and traffic lights put in. Incidentally, that is not a policeman in the middle of the road above Hills' lorry, but an unwary and timid pedestrian who has been there for about seven hours! In the foreground we see the inevitable roadworks, this time consisting of barrels which may contain tar, or beer, or a mixture of both.

There are, thankfully, still parts of the country where the old practical jokes on road users are still to be found. In rural parts of East Anglia there are two special ones. First, the sign posts. These are still of the old fashioned 'You can move the arms around in any direction you fancy' type, and they have often been duly adjusted. But even more fun is the practice of giving you signs to a remote village, say Dennington, and then when you are in a maze of lanes, and still a mile or two away from it, it completely disappears from the sign posts and three new villages appear instead.

Equally amusing on very twisting rural roads, running between the fields, is the practice of marking every bend with a warning sign, however gentle it may be, until you have lulled the driver into a sense of false security. Then, at the end of a straight stretch of road, you fail to put a sign up for the acute bend that follows. It is such fun to count the number of tyre marks going into the field opposite!

Later in our period came the introduction of three lane roads. Some of these were especially lethal and tempting, with a centre lane which could be used by vehicles travelling in either direction, or both. They could become a sort of jousting challenge, the first one to duck back into his own lane is a chicken! As many drivers, as noted, were not good at estimating speeds and distances the resulting

149

When Motoring Was Fun

These two photographs show the dramatic effect of road improvement schemes on the landscape. The photo above shows the old Wobbly Wheel Garage at the foot of Telegraph Hill near Exeter. The second photo is taken from more or less the same spot after the dual carriageway was built in the late 1960s.

crashes were often horrific, and involved many careful drivers as well.

Then came the introduction of the three-lane road with two lanes in one direction, and use of the centre lane in the other direction only if clear. It was a small improvement, for at least you could apportion blame afterwards. Such three lane roads were often to be found on hills, in an attempt to allow faster vehicles to overtake going up a hill.

There is a beauty on the A303 in Wiltshire. I have seen a long procession of cars approach it, and as each reached the dual carriageway the driver pulled out into the outer lane. The leading car, seeing the hill ahead, was also stimulated to put his foot down, and give the followers a run for their money. The whole procession thus moved out one lane, and by the time they reached the arrows directing them back in at the top of the hill, the entire procession, including me, was in exactly the same order as it had been at the bottom of the hill!

Finally came the spread of genuine dual carriageways, which offered wonderful scope for lane changing without any signals, hogging of the outside lane by slow and sedate cars, and above all lorry races. As was pointed out recently if one lorry has a top speed of 55mph and the other 56mph it will take about a fortnight for one to pass the other,

and especially if the speeds are reversed as soon as they come to a gradient! It never occurs to the lorry being overtaken to reduce speed a little, as that would reduce the frustration for all the cars on the road.

Once one lorry has at last succeeded in passing another, there comes the ceremony of the lights. The victorious lorry will flash lights that signal in Morse 'Yah boo sucks!' while the vanquished lorry responds with flashes which mean 'Grrrr, just wait 'til next time we meet and I'm unladen.'

I could not resist putting in a series of pictures showing police and drivers signals from the good old days. My old tourer has the original semaphore signals, which are not very easy to see, especially from certain angles, so I try to be efficient and clear with my hand signals, which are much easier to give from an open car.

The police hand signals, rarely seen these days because of all the roundabouts and traffic lights, seem to have changed little. I have never seen the 'I am about to stop' signal, which could be mistaken for 'look at that rare bird flying overhead.' The other signals are more or less the ones in my own repertoire today, so no great surprises there.

Early Days on the Open Road

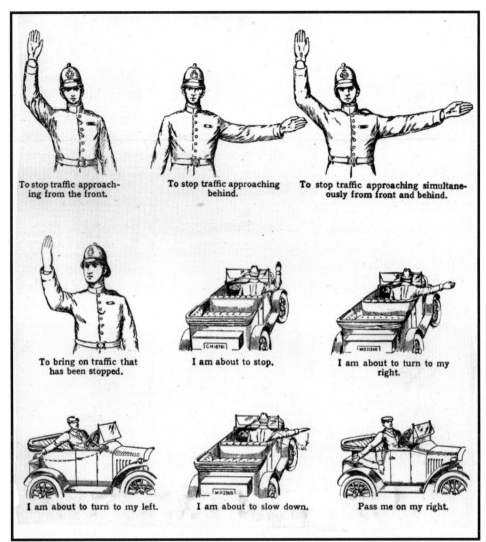

To stop traffic approaching from the front.

To stop traffic approaching behind.

To stop traffic approaching simultaneously from front and behind.

To bring on traffic that has been stopped.

I am about to stop.

I am about to turn to my right.

I am about to turn to my left.

I am about to slow down.

Pass me on my right.

Trying to get every potential motorist to use the trains instead has been a long running campaign. It took a very bad hit when Dr Beeching closed down most of the essential feeder lines, meaning that a huge part of the population had to get in their cars and drive several miles to the nearest mainline station. Many took the view that if they had to get their cars out to do that, and then try often in vain to find a parking place, and pay for it through the nose, then they might as well do the whole journey by car and be done with it, and thus save not only a rail fare or two, but the futile attempt to find a porter to help with heavy cases.

No one, however, proved that he was less equal to the challenge than the great Transport Supremo appointed in 1997, John Prescott. He vowed that he would get everyone back on the railways and buses in double quick time, while not actually offering to give up either of his own two Jaguar cars.

Much huffing and puffing and raised rail fares ensued, together with the cutting of bus services and record delays on trains. At last, ten years later, we were quietly allowed to learn the success of his highly paid endeavours. An extra four and a half million cars had been registered to run on Britain's roads! (And those were the ones whose owners had actually bothered to pay the tax!).

Anyone who drives out on the roads of today knows that the increases in traffic cannot go on, for if they do large areas of our road systems, and especially urban areas, will end up being completely gridlocked.

In our final picture in this chapter we see a busy scene at Blue Anchor railway station in the late 1930s. Already it is very hard to find anywhere to park your car, and the train is about to leave. (Just what the man on the wall is doing is hard to say, but it looks most uncomfortable and might easily lead to permanent disability!)

The station scene at Blue Anchor, near Carhampton, on a summers day in the late 1930s

Chapter 20

KEEPING ON TO THE END OF THE ROAD

A powerful car heads out along the seafront at Sidmouth, Devon. Women drivers have often been the butt of humour regarding their driving. But lower insurance premiums prove their safer driving habits.

It seems very appropriate to be starting to write this last chapter about our transports of delight on the day it is announced that Ford (an American Company) have just sold Jaguar and Land Rover, (two of our most famous British marques) to Tata (an Indian company!). I am sure that both John Prescott and Arthur Scargill will be joining me in mourning. Meanwhile I look forward to the new 4x4 Lada, with pedal-it-yourself green credentials, a cardboard body and a price tag of £999!

I think it was really my generation that thought it had won the war, and then watched through the 50s and 60s as USA, Germany, France and Japan stripped us of all our prestigious industries while we were so bankrupt and exhausted by our war effort that we were powerless to resist. They also had a lot of help from our Trades Unions, of course. Trades Union leaders of that period have a lot of answering to do both to the nation and even more to their own members, whose jobs they destroyed.

My generation began to look back with nostalgic longing to the time when Britain was a great nation, and produced vehicles, among many other things, that were admired and used all over the world.

Preserving old vehicles as a hobby goes back a long way, of course, as the annual London to Brighton run reminds us. But the 'Old Crocks race' was regarded as the fad of a rather small and nutty group of fanatics, as exemplified in the immortal film 'Genevieve.' Apart from that most people were too busy trying to keep an old family car on the road to have much time for the restoration of obsolete vehicles.

In the late 1960s, however, this wave of nostalgia seems to have taken hold, and we started the great preservation movement. It coincided with the end of steam traction on Britain's railways, and the saving of many wonderful locomotives from the notorious scrap yard at Barry.

This was the period when many museums were started, preserving everything from aircraft to barrel organs to domestic furniture and cooking utensils, and some wonderful dolls houses. You don't get much smaller than that! And then there were the multitude of vehicles.

As recorded, I stumbled into car restoration entirely by accident, and the experience opened up a whole new world to me. I soon discovered that all over the country there were an incredible variety of

Retrieving Tess, the author's Sunbeam Talbot: Top left: *The start of a project, bringing Tess to her new home, c.1989.* Top right: *Tess in the car port spray booth receiving a new coat of paint.* Centre: *Tess restored and ready for wedding car duty, poses with some of the restoration team and friends.*

man and women dedicated to restoring, preserving and running their old vehicles.

There is a lot to be said for this hobby. The drivers of old cars do a very low mileage in them, so that their 'carbon footprint' is very small, much less than that of a healthy cow!

The hobby is relatively cheap. The cars cost nothing to tax, and little to insure. Most maintenance work on them is done by their owners, or very skilled specialist mechanics who do not have the overheads of large garages.

It is a very sociable hobby, with flourishing owners clubs, who hold regular meetings and publish magazines which keep members in touch with what is going on.

Above all, it brings a lot of satisfaction. The moment ones drives out of the garage in the restored car, running again 'under its own steam,' is a moment to savour. Much time and not a little skill will have been put into the project, - in our case by most of the members of the family. And restoration can be done in any private garage, or even as in our case in a car port. When it comes to restoration I have always found other owners who were experts having done the job already, and who were always very generous with their time and expertise when I had a particular problem I couldn't solve.

It is important to have space under cover for the operation, and to bear in mind that it will often take months not weeks, and even a couple of years in some cases. The older cars were often made out of a combination of wood and steel, the frames being frequently made of ash wood. This can be quite a problem, and involves carpentry skills, but again it is often possible to buy the necessary wood pieces ready for assembly.

There are, of course, some specialist jobs that you cannot do yourself, like re-chroming bumpers and other parts. These will have to be sent away, but there are a number of workshops that specialise in this, and it is wonderfully exciting when the chromed parts come back looking as good as new.

The car port adapted as a paint spraying booth for Alberta, the 1½ litre Riley in 1988.

Part of a huge camp for Riley cars and their owners at their National Rally. Mid 1990s.

Painting is always something of a challenge, and in particular choosing a colour. In the case of Tess, my Sunbeam Talbot, the factory produced her in four colours, black, steel grey, gunmetal blue, and carnadine, a sort of awful violet/purple! We did a bit or research, and discovered that if you placed a special order, and paid an extra £1.17.6d, you could have your new car sprayed any colour you liked, so we decided that as Tess is a very 'eye-catching' sort of car, we would go for pre-war MG red! She looks very good in this colour, and she certainly catches the eye!

Soon after her restoration was completed, the owners club, which is the Sunbeam Talbot Alpine Register, or STAR, decided to organise a hill climb event not too far away, and we went to take part. I did once or twice wonder what on earth I was doing charging up hills and across fields in my newly restored treasure! Tess in fact seemed to thoroughly enjoy the experience, and took second prize.

All through the summer months the owners clubs and other organisations organise events for classic cars. These can vary from the Ipswich to Felixstowe run, with over four hundred vehicles of every type taking part, to small displays of a few vehicles at a village Fete. Rallies and treasure hunts are always popular, as are visits to museums and stately homes. If you live fairly centrally, and have a classic car that can cope with modern traffic conditions, you can fill your calendar with two events every weekend if you have a mind to do so, and can afford the petrol!

Tess and a friend wait for their turn at the hill climb event in 1990.

As Tess and Polly will testify, older cars like a warm snug garage. Late 1990s.

Tess on parade at the Sunbeam Talbot stand at Colchester Classic car show. Late 1990s.

In this country there are a number of professional car restorers, and I am very fortunate to live close to one of them, Michael Ladd. Michael has a 'stable' of about eight classic cars that he has restored, and has two more 'on the go,' one a veteran model. He entered the national competition to restore a Ford Model T Tourer in a specified time and to a given budget, as seen on the previous page, and won first prize. One of his other cars which he has brilliantly restored is a Maxwell Tourer, also seen on the following pages.

Driving the old cars can be quite a challenge. Michael did not dare let me loose on the Model T Ford, as its controls are so different to any other more modern car. Even the challenge of the huge gear lever travel in Tess can be a bit daunting, and even embarrassing as reverse gear is located somewhere between the front passengers legs. This can sometimes require hasty explanation!

In a vintage car you have to manipulate three pedals, including double de-clutching, use the indicator switch, steer and give hand signals all to do a right turn off a main road! Sometimes you run out of hands and have to 'hold' the steering wheel momentarily with your knee!

In this country we are incredibly lucky to have many motor museums with wonderful collections of old vehicles dating back into the 1880s. Chief among these is the National Motor Museum at Beaulieu in Hampshire, which was founded and developed by Lord Montagu of Beaulieu. Here is to be found not only a wonderful collection of vehicles representing the whole development of transport, but also some world famous racing cars and other cars which have been preserved for future generations

Throughout the country one will find large and small museums, sometimes run commercially, sometimes mainly by volunteers. Some have been started by an individual with his own collection (it does appear to be mainly a man's thing!) some by a group. Large cities like Glasgow will have a museum run by the city council, and in this case it covers rail and sea as well as road transport, and is a superb collection.

The Model T Ford arrives in Michael Ladd's worshop ready for the competition. 2005.

Michael Ladd at the wheel of his restored prizewinning Model T Ford, with the admiring author, in 2008.

Early Days on the Open Road

Mick Ladd's restored Maxwell Tourer ready for the Ipswich to Felixstowe Run in 2008.

A beautifully restored tram on a cobbled street at the Beamish Museum, Durham in the 1970s.

The Beamish Open Air Museum in Durham has trams giving rides to visitors, as does the national Tram museum at Crich in Derbyshire. The collection here is a wonderful history of the work of trams down the years. Or you can ride on the miniature trams of the Seaton Tramway.

On my recent visit to the Glasgow Transport Museum I found myself staring at a wicker picnic basket in a glass cabinet. It was my mother's incredible model, as detailed on page 136, but it was about two thirds the size, and intended as a travelling Tea Set for use on trains. Our was larger as it had all the crockery as well!

Another most important feature of Classic Car Owners clubs is that many operate a spares section, and an owner in trouble can ring up the spares secretary, and the required part will be in the post within hours, - and at a reasonable cost.

It should also be noted that our old cars are far more robust than their modern counterparts. On my Ford Focus the flywheel has just failed and fallen to pieces after a mere 43 000 miles! I reckon that the flywheel on Tess has done between two hundred and three hundred thousand miles! My Mk V Cortina did 250 000 miles on one flywheel!

157

When Motoring Was Fun

Travelling Tea Set, in wickerwork case, on display in Glasgow Transport Museum 2008.

Moreover, a new flywheel for the Focus cost £1240 to repair, with no help whatever from Ford, which sum of money would keep Tess going happily for many years!

Our classic cars do not just occupy a snug garage and go on the occasional fine weather Rally when inclination occurs. Many work quite hard for their living, both as wedding cars and as cars featuring in films set in the past. Others will go on display to enhance fund raising events, both large and small. And proud owners put in many hours keeping them up to the mark.

In addition to the large number of fairly ordinary cars which have been preserved, a number of very rare and interesting models have also survived, together with a fascinating selection of passenger carrying buses, trams and coaches, many motorcycles, and a staggering variety of commercial vehicles of every description.

As I have suggested, I do not know of any other country in the world which treasures it's Transports of Delight in the way that Britain has done. The vehicles show not only the development of transport, much of it the products of British designers and engineers, but they are also a remarkable commentary on the social history of our country in the years c 1880 to 1960.

I have tried in this book to combine a survey, albeit shallow, of the development of passenger carrying vehicles over the period covered, with the effect they had in the changing of outlook and ways of life for many, and also to record that the experience of these old vehicles brought a spirit of both fun and adventure to their owners and passengers. The adventures might not always be free from minor frustrations at the time, but they would be the subject of a good story told at the dinner table, slightly embellished, later in the day!

A Model T Ford, well polished for wedding duty, waits outside a church c.1988.

The sublime...

...to the ridiculous.

Two forms of transport that could hardly be further apart. The 1909 Rolls Royce tourer in all its glory, is considered by many to be the ultimate in combining top engineering with truly sumptuous motoring. The lower picture, taken in Crediton, Devon, around 1880, shows a group of boys admiring a tricycle contraption designed by local man, Mr Dicker. The boy on the left holds the ultimate in environmentally friendly personal transport – an iron hoop to be bowled along the road.

*View from the back seat, over the author's shoulder,
as Tess wanders down a country road.*